Living

LIVING THROUGH THE CONFLICT
Belfast oral histories

A Pieces of the Past project

Published in 2014 by
Dúchas oral history archive
©2014 The contributors and
Dúchas oral history archive

ISBN 978-0-9930521-0-1
First Edition
First impression

Dúchas Oral History Archive
Falls Community Council
275 - 277 Falls Road
Belfast
BT12 6FD
T. 02890202030
[e] archive@fallscouncil.com
[w] www.duchasarchive.com

Designed by Factotum, Belfast
Printed by Print Library, Belfast
Cover image by David Haughey

All right reserved. No part of this publication may be reproduced, stored in a retrieval system or transmitted in any form or by any means, electronic, mechanical, photocopying, scanning, recording or otherwise, without the prior written permission of the copyright owners and publisher of this book.

The authors have asserted their right under the Copyright Designs and Patents Act 1988, to be identified as author of this work. A catalogue record for this book is available from the British Library and the National Library of Ireland

CONTENTS

Introduction	....	7
I was born… Rugadh mé	....	11
Stories Scéalta	....	41
Process	....	113
Index	....	121

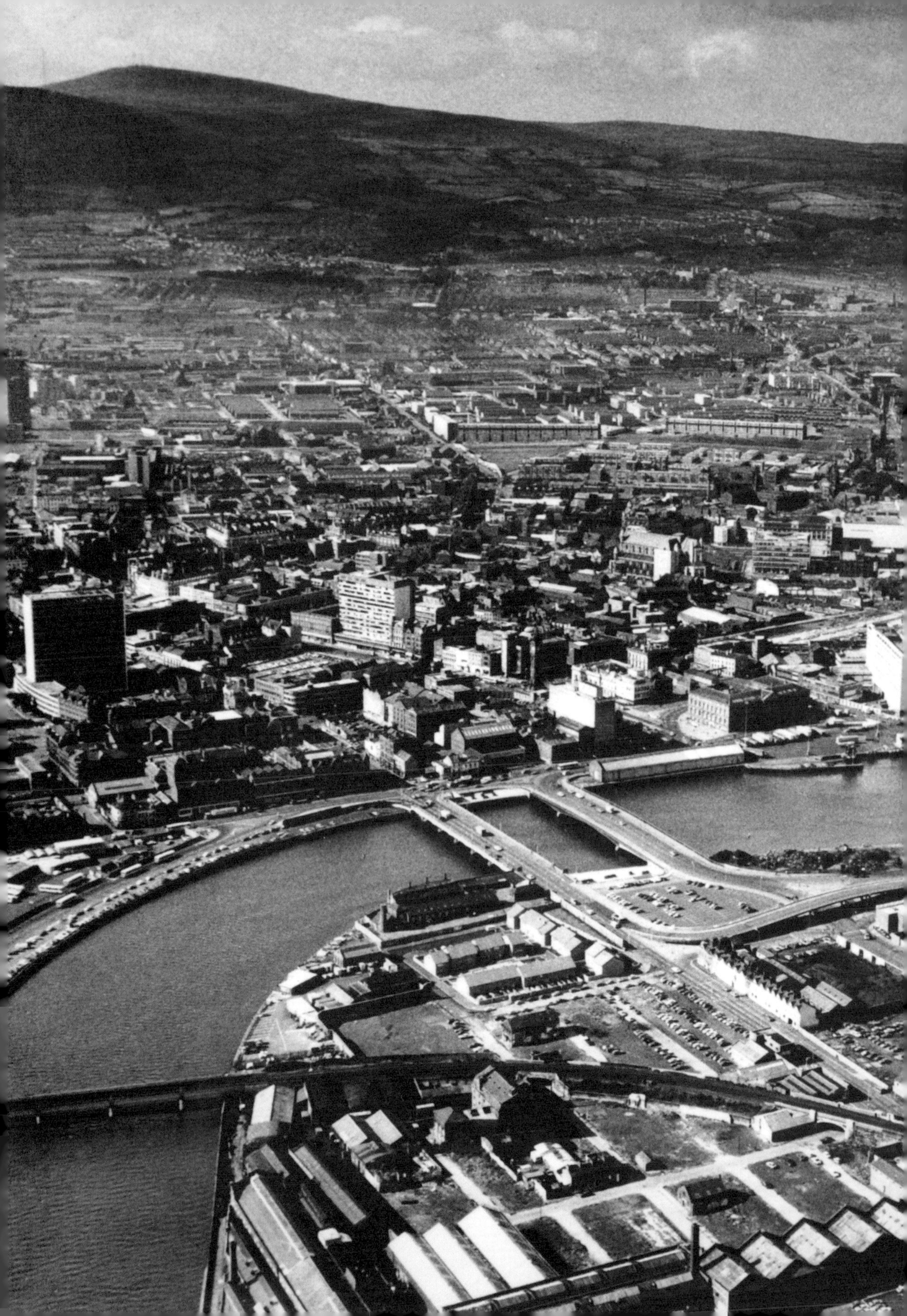

LIVING THROUGH THE CONFLICT
Belfast oral histories

INTRODUCTION

Background

This book is made up of oral history accounts of living through the conflict in Northern Ireland / the North of Ireland. Between 2012 and 2014 over 100 interviews were gathered through the Pieces of the Past project and the book is a compilation of extracts from these interviews. Pieces of the Past is a partnership of six organisations working with the Falls Community Council's oral history archive Dúchas. The partner organisations come from across the city of Belfast: Shankill Women's Centre, Epic, Forbairt Feirste, Charter NI, Fáilte Feirste Thiar and Belfast Taxis Community Interest Company. Another organisation, Shankill Area Social History joined the project at a later stage to do training and collect interviews. This is a diverse partnership. The organisations span the east and west of the city and all come from working class unionist or nationalist communities. These communities are among those that experienced the impact of the conflict most heavily over the three decades since 1969 until the ceasefires in the mid-90s. Indeed, as some of the interviews in this book demonstrate, the communities have continued to experience violence and trauma during the transition from armed conflict in the last two decades. The journey towards a peaceful society is ongoing and dealing with the legacy of the conflict is a process with many challenges and setbacks. The Pieces of the Past project has not been easy, but commitment, leadership and courage from all the partners, volunteers, staff and contributors has enabled all the oral histories to be collected and held together in one archive and to be shared in this publication.

Structure of the book

The interviews are set out in two main sections. The first section is entitled I was born and gives an extract from the start of each interview. This gives an impression of the family background of each contributor. These extracts are set out in alphabetical order and have a reference number to indicate where the reader can find another extract from this contributor. The next section entitled Stories contains selected narratives from the oral history interviews. They are arranged in a roughly chronological order and span several decades, some before the outbreak of the conflict, the majority during the conflict and some about the period of the peace process. The final part of the book is called Process and this gives more detail about the development of the project and introduces all those who played a role in gathering and archiving the interviews. There is an index listing the names of the contributors along with the person that interviewed them and the supporting organisation. The 18 interviews that were gathered through Forbairt Feirste were carried out in Irish and there is a translation into English following each extract from these interviews.

The narratives

The short narratives that sit beside each other in this book are extracts from a longer oral history interview carried out with each contributor. The interviews range in length from 20 minutes to 3 hours. For most contributors at least two selections were made, one from the start of the interview situating each person in their family history and the other, an extract from later on in the interview. There has been no attempt by the editors to look for overarching or connecting themes. What guided the interview selection was what caught the attention or lingered in the memory. There was also thought given to what the contributor might want to be taken from their interview. It was sometimes very difficult to select one extract so more were chosen. Sometimes what made the selection difficult was that the interaction with the interviewer was so interwoven that it was hard to separate out one section. Even where there are longer or multiple extracts what was chosen does not convey the immediacy and complexity of the full oral history interview. This book of interview excerpts gives only a glimpse into the oral history interviews. The full content of all those interviews covers more than 100 hours of recording and 2000 pages of transcript. Another way to look at this book is to see it as a catalogue of the interviews which gives a taste of the depth and breadth of the rich stories told. The sense of a catalogue is reinforced by the fact that the extracts are presented without interpretation or any overarching context. There are however many themes that can be discerned in these narratives and it is hoped that these can be explored in future publications from this oral history work.

Partnership

The Pieces of the Past partnership grew from a pilot project between the Dúchas archive and Charter NI in 2010 supported by Belfast City Council's EU Peace 3 programme. When this proved successful the partnership expanded to become the seven organisations of Pieces of the Past. The project set up a steering group composed of representatives of the organisations that make up Pieces of the Past along with the project staff guiding and managing the oral history work. Our initial meetings spent a lot of time testing the ground and building trust before embarking on the interview gathering. We created a mission statement together. The conversations that created the environment for the interview collection and archiving have been private and public. All of the work involved in this project has involved hundreds of people at many levels. Oral history work is at the heart of this project and so also is conflict resolution.

Methodology

It was decided to train oral history volunteers to carry out the interviews. The organisations in the steering group recruited the volunteer interviewers who came from the communities that were interviewed. The project staff trained them in the oral history methodology used in the Dúchas archive. This adopts a life history approach starting each interview with a question on when the person was born and their family background. The interview unfolds depending on each contributor's circumstances and experience. The themes that are usually covered in an interview include childhood, leisure, politics, religion, schooling, working life, later family life as well as experiences of the conflict and peace process. The training also emphasises the importance of explaining the process to the contributor, including the choices involved in the deposit of the interview in the archive and uses of the interview. All of the recorded interviews are transcribed. Transcripts are only lightly edited and remain faithful to the recording. A copy of the recording and transcript is returned to the contributor and at that point they decide if they are content to deposit their interview in the Dúchas archive.

After the training the interviewers sought out contributors and were often helped in this by the partner organisations. Sometimes the interviewers knew the person well and sometimes not at all. At times the interviewers were brought back together for meetings to discuss issues and dilemmas and also to enable broader political discussions. This brought the volunteers into a conflict resolution group process similar to what was happening in the steering group.

The Dúchas archive

The Dúchas oral history archive was set up in 1999 to record the experience of the conflict. The initial focus of the archive was on the community of nationalist West Belfast but from an early stage there were efforts to also collect experiences from people in other communities situated differently in relation to the conflict. Falls Community Council envisaged the Dúchas archive as a tool for learning and for conflict resolution as well as leaving a legacy to the future. Over the last number of years of the peace process there began to be more opportunities for working in partnership with other community groups in Belfast. As described above, a model was developed for working in partnership and gathering interviews. This involved training oral history interviewers but also crucially creating spaces for discussion and conversation. Dúchas has created a digital archive where visitors can browse through the collection. The interviews can be listened to or read and the visitor can see the whole interaction between interviewer and contributor. The archive is not available online although aspects of the collection and the work can be accessed from the website (www.duchasarchive.com). There are currently over 100 interviews in the archive with another 150 in the process of being archived and deposited. Each of the organisations involved in Pieces of the Past has their own collection in the Dúchas archive. The translation of the Irish word Dúchas is 'heritage' or 'the experiences that make us what we are'. Here are some pieces about who we are.

I WAS BORN...
RUGADH'S TOGADH MÉ

_____

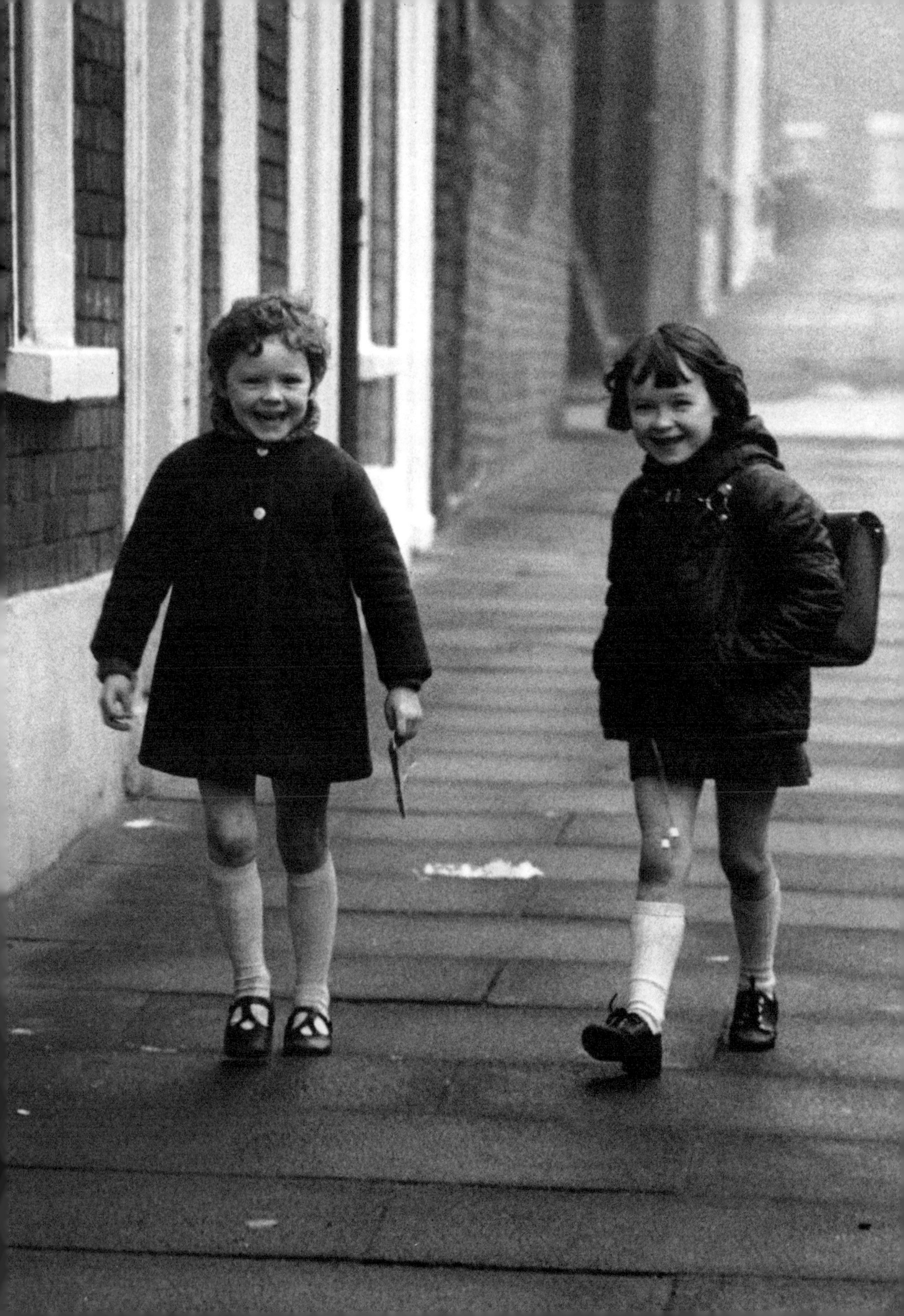

Mark Anderson – 88, 97, 106

I was born in Holywood 1983. I have two brothers, a sister that passed away at an early age, and then another sister. My sister who died was two years of age. She died in a house fire in 1986. She actually started the house fire in the early hours of the morning. She woke up and went down stairs; she got a box of matches and started the fire. Only for our dog, our labrador, that woke my mother up, there is the possibility that none of the family would be here today. My mother got up and got us up and got us out of the house. My young sister, we couldn't find her. The fire brigade was called; the fire brigade couldn't find her. It was actually a next door neighbour that went into the house and found her in the kitchen, on one of the chairs. Unfortunately she passed away in hospital. I was only four. My mother was bringing us up by herself because my dad was actually in jail at the time. He was let out for the funeral on day release, but after that he was put back in again. So it was hard on us and hard on my mother as well.

Samuel Aughey – 15

I was born in January 1942 in Richmond Street on the Shankill Road. I'm a Hammer boy born. My mother was a Hammer girl, she came from Ariel Street. So my granny lived 50 yards away from us when we were in Richmond Street. My father was a Crumlin Road man from Leopold Street. When they first got married my mum had been a mill girl in Greeves' Mill on the Falls Road. My father had left school at 15 and moved into Mackie's. And he didn't leave Mackie's until 50 years later, 65 he retired. So my father was a 50 year man with Mackie's, all his days. As I say, I was born on the Shankill, and my family are Shankill people. But we moved to Ardoyne, which was a new estate then when I was about four. After we moved to Ardoyne my sister was born and then 2 younger brothers.

Anne Barkley – 36

I was born in Dublin in 1939 in the Rotunda Hospital, and I lived in Dublin until I was 6 months old. Until my mother died, my mother died of TB on Christmas day 1939. My sister also died, you called her Mary, and she died of TB. That's the time the TB was very bad in the south. And I came and my father couldn't cope and me and my brother were put into a home in Dublin. So one of my aunts in County Wicklow, outside Arklow, they had a big farm, and she wanted to take my brother but she wouldn't take me, and my aunt in Pomeroy just decided that she would take me.

Eileen Bell – 2

I was born in August 1943 in Dromara, County Down. I shouldn't have been born there as I was due in September but I decided to come early. I was born very premature for that time, very premature. The doctor said to my father that I should be christened or baptised as quickly as possible because I wasn't going to last the night. I was 3, just touching 4 lbs. I was kept alive - they had an old range – one side was the fire and the other side was the oven. So that kept me warm – an early incubator! My Aunt Lily, who was my god-mother, put the griddle on the side of the fire and put me on it with towels and kept me alive that way.

My mother died in 1954 which changed all our lives because she was a very, very dominant woman. She was, though, also very loving. My father was heart broken when my mother died. It was a Darby and Joan marriage.

Girls coming home from school, Shankill Road area (1972)
Oliver Morris, Hulton Archive

Jean Boyce

I was born in 1929 in 89 Crimea Street in my grandfather's house. My mother lived there for a few years and then she got a house in Loftus Street and we lived there. I always remember my grandfather had pigs in the back, he kept pigs for a living. Then he mended boots and he gave the pigs up. My father, he was a great footballer. But he got so many wettings, playing football, he got pneumonia and it turned to TB. He was only 28 when he died. So I was only two years and ten months when my father died and my sister was only 13 months. My mother was a spinner in the mill. Then she started work in the shipyard cleaning offices. So she worked until my sister and I started work and then she left. I started work in the mill at 14. I left school on a Wednesday, and I was in the mill on a Thursday in the reel room.

Seanna Breathnach – 99

Rugadh mé in Ard Eoin i '56 agus ansin togadh mé sa Trá Ghearr. Déanta na fírinne, bhog muid go dtí ceantar protastúnach ag tús na seascaidí agus ba ghnách liom crochadh thart le daoine ón Trá Ghearr, de thairbhe go raibh seanmháthair s'agam ina cónaí ann go fóill. Nuair a thosaigh an choimhlint, maraíodh fear óg, a bhí cairdiúil linn, Caitliceach óg, maraíodh é ar leac a dhorais.

I was born in Ardoyne in '56 and then I was raised in Short Strand. To tell you the truth, we moved to a Protestant area in the beginning of the sixties and I used to hang around with people from Short Strand, because my grandmother still lived there. When the conflict started, a young man was killed who was friendly to us, a young Catholic, he was killed on his doorstep.

Danny Brown – 89

Tháinig mé ar an tsaol ar an dara lá is fiche de Feabhra, 1955 i Sráid Kampar. Níor rugadh mé san otharlann, rugadh mé sa teach. Níl ann dó níos mó, leagadh an ceantar uilig ach tá an mhainistreach, an clochar agus an comhar creidmheasa ann, agus an pub, deir sin cuid mhór. Nuair a phós mo mháthair agus m'athair, bhí mo mháthair ag obair i Muileann Greeves agus bhí m'athair ag obair mar sclábhaí ar na bóithre. Obair shealadach a bhí sa sclábhaíocht ach fuair sé post buan, ní post maith, ní raibh airgead riamh againn, ach fuair sé post mar bus conductor. Fuair sé i dtrioblóid cúpla uair leis an chomhlacht mar bhí baint aige leis na ceardchumainn.

I came into the world on the twenty-second of February, 1955 in Cawnpore Street. I wasn't born in the hospital, I was born at home. It isn't there anymore, the whole area was knocked down but the monastery, the convent and the credit union are still there, and the pub, that says a lot. When my mother and father got married, my mother was working in Greeves' Mill and my father was working as a labourer on the roads. Labouring was temporary work but he got a permanent job, not a good job, we never had money, but he got a job as a bus conductor. He got in trouble a few times with the company because he was involved in the trade unions.

Breige Brownlee – 45, 78, 87

I was born in the Royal Victoria Hospital in Belfast in 1959. I have five brothers and three sisters and I am the second youngest. My dad was a bus man and my mum was a cleaner. My mum, Mary Adams, came from Varna Street and my dad, Jamsie Brownlee, came from the Whiterock. They were both members of the Republican movement. My mum is 91 now and she was one of the last Cumann na Mban members. She was involved in the 40s and 50s onward.

Joe Burns – 84, 104

I was born in 1937. There was 12 of us. Six boys and six girls. It was the happiest childhood in anybody's life, because we all looked after one another. I had no interest in school. All I ever wanted to do was go over to the bog meadows and play, and get lost in the bog meadows. I left school at 14. The first job when I left school was in a wine factory on the Lisburn Road at the top of Tates Avenue. Stuck that for two /three years. Then I left that and went to the house repairing. I worked actually in Browns Square, at the bottom of the Shankill. And actually what we done then it was just a cart, maybe a ton of sand, and a half a ton of stones and cement, and you pushed that up the Shankill Road to do repairs on the houses.

Sean Carmichael – 76, 101

I was born in the Royal Victoria Hospital. I have three brothers and two sisters. My mother is from Northwick Drive in Ardoyne. She was a stitcher in Flax Mill. My father came from Cullingtree Road, the Pound Loney. He was a glazier. He worked for McMullans in Smithfield. I attended Holy Cross boys primary school and then went on to St Gabriel's.

Kevin Carson – 5, 54

I was born on 13th February 1952 in a place called Puala, a suburb of Valetta in Malta. My mother and father were both in the RAF, and they were both stationed in Malta in the Mediterranean. The rest of my brothers and sisters were born when we moved to North Green in Andersonstown. I was the oldest. Well, the oldest living. I had an elder sister that died at child birth. It's still a great source of anguish, for members of the family, trying to track down where her remains are. I assume that my sister was actually born still birth in Malta. We're still trying to track down the details from the hospital archives because when the Brits pulled out they took all the files with them. So somewhere in Kew Gardens in England are all the records, if they did keep records of still births in them days.

David Colvin – 64

I was born in North Belfast, Tigers Bay, in 1958. The household was myself, my young brother and my mother. My father had cleared off once my young brother was born. I went to the local primary school which was Currie Primary School. And everything was alright until I turned ten when my mother was caught in a bomb blast in Gallagher's and that sort of …. she took serious epileptic fits after it and her right arm where the gate had fell on her. I lost my childhood then. It split the family up. The brother, he left home and he went to live with the other aunt. I went to work at ten years of age after school to support the family. It was straight in from school, jeans on, and away to work in the chippy, maybe work there till about eleven o'clock at night. That was five days a week, and then on a Saturday I would have worked in the scrap yard, and then when I was off school at holiday I worked full time in the scrap yard.

Bobby Connolly – 49

I was born in 1939. I have four brothers and one sister. I'm from Hannahstown. Mountainy men, that's what people called us, they mostly called us mountainy men. I went to school in Hannahstown, on the hill. The school's gone now. My father and mother were farmers and we all worked on the land when we were at school. If there was something to do on the farm you didn't go to school. That's the way it was. School was more or less part time. The farm was about 40 acres, a small farm. You had to be up in the morning about half five to milk the cows, and the milkman came at nine o'clock, and if you hadn't it ready for him he'd go on without you.

Tracey Coulter – 111

I was born in Belfast on September 26th, 1978. There's four of us, Jackie's the oldest, I'm the next. Then there's Natalie, and then Amy. My parents were Agnes and Jackie Coulter. We lived up in Ainsworth Avenue and it was quite close to the Springfield Road so there was a wee 'Road Closed' sign barrier. That's all we had dividing Protestants and Catholics. It was. It was scary now, it definitely was. I remember I always used to think everybody was going to come into our houses and that we were all going to get burnt to death, or we were going to get shot because all you heard was constant shooting. And then there were times, like around the likes of July and band season and things like that, it would have got really more tense.

Geraldine Crawford – 58

I was born in the Royal Victoria Hospital and was the eighth child to Bridget and Ned Crawford. Two younger sisters were born after me so there were 8 girls and 2 boys in the family. We lived in a 2 up and 2 down house off the Falls Road near the Falls Baths. We learned to swim and got our weekly bath there. My father was a fishmonger and then went to work on the docks at the Heysham port in England. During my early life my father was mostly out of work. He was big into the Transport and General Workers union. My mother worked at cleaning jobs and during the summer holidays we would go with her to work which we didn't like. She cleaned the Banker's Club which was above Lilley & Skinner shoe shop in Donegal Place.

Colin Curragh – 113

I was born in Dundonald hospital in 1974. I lived in Emerald Street there, just off the Woodstock Road. So I lived there from an early age right through to about 10. From 10 onwards I ended up in Donaghadee. My Da worked in the shipyard and he took early redundancy. So he took his redundancy money and bought a house in Donaghadee and shipped us all down there. He took us down there, more or less, to keep me out of trouble.

Jayne Davidson – 100

I was born in 1961, the middle child, the oldest girl, two older boys, three girls. I went to Wheatfield School and then I moved on to Everton. I'd passed my 11+ but I'd decided not to go to the Model. I'd hid my results so that I could go with my chums. Alliance Parade, where I was born, was mixed, it was a mixed street. Alliance Parade got a quare bit in the Troubles, you know, between bombs and that. But I wasn't aware of anything until I remember my close friends being there one night and then the next day, vanished.

Kieran Devlin – 60
I was born in 1956 in Carrick Hill, but I was only there a lock of months and then my parents moved up into Locan Street in Beechmount. So that's where I grew up till I got married and moved up to Dermott Hill, and that's been me ever since. I haven't moved. I don't believe in moving. My mother would have cleaned different wee shops in Donegal Arcade. My Da was a docker, and he would have went out and worked away and drunk away like all dockers do. So a lot of the times I had to go down to the docks to go into a bar to take money off him to give to my Ma.

Owen Doherty – 72
I was born in 1939 in Belfast. My father was a stonemason. There were nine of us in the family.

John Dougan – 112
I was born in August 1971, and I was born and lived in Wigton Street on the Shankill Road for the first few months of my life. From Wigton Street I went to Glencairn and stayed in Glencairn until I was 15 years of age. Glencairn, to me, was a world away from the Shankill. Growing up in Glencairn we had no need to venture down the Shankill. You were took down every 12th. The 12th was the mainstay for us all, and we were took down to the bar at the bottom of the Shankill and all the men gave you the big 50ps. You always looked forward to getting the big 50ps before going to watch the parade. You went up to Clifton Street Orange Hall and watched them all amalgamating. All getting together, and then we would've went down into the town to watch them walking by. That was the main time you got out of Glencairn.

Beatrice Elliott – 25
I was born on the Shankill Road, Mountjoy Street. There was seven in my family, my three brothers and one sister, my mother and father. It was a one up, one down house, there was only one bedroom. We were very poor. I went to Mayo Street School Primary first, and then when I came eleven I went over to Glenwood Intermediate. It was called Glenwood Intermediate on the Shankill Road. I was there till I was fifteen. I left school on a Friday and started work on Monday up in Ewart's Weaving Factory, learning the weaving. You had to go to the Training School for six weeks to learn the looms, how to weave.

Harry Enright – 12
I was born in 1931 in Upton Street in Carrick Hill. And we left Upton Street when I was 5 to move to Beechmount Avenue, beside the Clowney River which was then open. It's been closed over since and houses put on it. And we lived in Beechmount Avenue for five years, and then, because there was too much traffic and it was too near Kennedy's Bakery, we moved to Beechmount Crescent which was the last street to be built. We were all born at home and I was the third of five children, but Mona, my eldest sister, died from a heart complaint when she was 5. Beechmount was a new addition to the parish, and it was built above clay pits where the fields had all been excavated to get the clay for making bricks. Those pits stretched from Beechmount right up to the Whiterock, and

they were very deep. I reckon they were one hundred foot deep in some places. And they had pools of water that were used to swim in. But also for fights between Beechmount and Whiterock. Because if you went through anybody else's territory you were going to be pulled.

Seamus Finucane – 32

I was born in 1957. We're a Falls Road family from Sevastopol Street - that's where we grew up in our formative years and where our childhood memories would emanate from. My father lived in Divis Street and my mother hailed from the New Lodge. At one stage they lived in Wall Street, Carrick Hill. We're a family of ten, counting mother and father. Seven boys and one girl. I'm the third youngest son. My father tied down two jobs most of his life. He was a barman by trade, but he also worked as a labourer in the flour mills that were prominent in the city at this time. My mother was primarily a housewife but turned her hand to working in stalls – fruit stalls and clothes stalls. I suppose you could say she had a bit of business acumen.

Gerry Fitzpatrick – 37

I was born in Cawnpore Street, Belfast, off the Kashmir Road, 73 years ago. My father, he worked in the brickyard over in Beechmount. And he had a shop, it was a shop and a house together. My father and mother worked in the shop, you know, and tried to rear a family too. Basically when he came home he went into the shop to let my mother out, to give her a bit of a breather. She was working all day in the shop. The two of them tried to work it evenly. I went to St. Galls off Waterville Street and I left school when I was 14.

Micky Gallagher – 8, 13

I was born in 1945. I'm actually a twin. I've a twin sister and we're the youngest of ten. We lived in 32 Locan Street and I was born in the house. It was ten feet by eight feet, and there was twelve of us in it with two bedrooms. You went into the bedroom and there was two big double beds and a chest of drawers, and 4 in one bed and three in the other. And you went into the front room and there was a bed for my mother and father, then a big curtain drew across the middle and a bed for my three sisters. The jaw box was out the back as we called it, an outside toilet and outside washing. But sure, it didn't matter whether you were from the Shankill or Falls, everybody lived in them conditions then, you know what I mean, in wee small rooms.

Sandra Gibney – 18

I was born in 1961. I've always lived on the Shankill. My first address was in Blaney Street, off Agnes Street. My father was Alec Gibney, he was a baker. My mum was Rachel and she worked in various wee jobs cleaning and stuff, and her last job was in Halls Bridge factory till it closed. I'm the oldest of three. I have a brother Andrew and a sister Alison. I was actually christened in Falls Road Methodist Church, me and my brother and sister. So it wasn't as closed off then by peace walls and all as it would be now. We lived in Blaney Street until I was about 15. My first school was Blenheim Primary school and I was there until Primary 4 and then you moved over to Hensworth, it's now Malvern

Primary. It was Hensworth when I went to it, you called it the Hen House.

Irene Glassey – 28, 114
I was born in March 1954 at half seven in the morning. I was the fourth child. I had two older sisters and an older brother, and then there was a sister born after me. My mother came from the country, a wee place outside Killyleagh called Shrigley. My grandfather was a chauffeur for the mill owner, and my mum and her sisters and brother lived in, like a lodge, at the bottom of the garden. They moved up to Belfast then to live in Dunmurry Lane, then she went to work in the mill and then she met my daddy. My daddy comes from the Shankill Road, from Riga Street. I grew up in Highfield estate which is just up the road and I went to school in Springhill Primary School.

Liz Groves – 7, 80
I was born in 1945 in a house that I lived in until I got married, in Lepper Street on the Antrim Road. My da was a bookie and my ma always ran wee corner shops. Belfast was one of the most safe, most wonderful cities to grow up at that time. We played in a park called Queen Mary's Garden in Alexandra Park on the Antrim Road. I also played in a park called Castleton, down off North Queen Street. They were all in a kind of a cluster and you didn't go into them from the 1st July right through to the end of August because you would have been beaten.

Roy Harris – 47, 56
I am 70 and I was born in Ardgowan Street on the Castlereagh Road, and I went to Euston Street School and then, when I was 11 years of age, I went to Dundonald, Orangefield. People think the Troubles started in 1969, but when we were only young kids, at 16 years of age, going to the Plaza, you had to fight your way out of it. Even then. It's not the first time I had to run out of the Plaza and jump onto a tram, because it was trams at that time, the trolleys with electric wires. I remember at 17 years of age a fella saying to me about going to a dance in Coaches Street on the Falls Road, and we couldn't have been in it any more than 10 minutes and we were chased down the Falls Road. And there was a dance at the bottom of the Woodstock Road called Mitchells, and I even meet people right now that actually met in Mitchells. And if you'd have gone into Mitchells with a Roman Catholic you'd have got kicked down the stairs. And that was when I was only 17, 18 years of age.

Jo-Ann Harrison – 39
I was born in Canmore Street, Shankill Road, September 1964. There were five in total, my mum and dad, and myself and two younger sisters. It was a small kitchen house, two up and two down, and an outside toilet. I can remember before the troubles started, playing out in the street in Canmore Street and on down to the bottom of Cupar Street. The streets were opened then and you played with Catholic children. I remember going on to the Falls Road with my mum, taking me to the Falls Park. I remember going in and out of Catholic homes, playing with the children. It was just all fun then, everyone just played together.

Tommy Harrison – 95
I was born in 1957 in Disraeli Street in the Woodvale area. There were five of us, myself,

mother and father, and two older sisters. We lived in a two-up, two-down, the usual kitchen house, no bathroom, outside toilet. They were poor days so it was pretty tight. There weren't many people used carpet then. There was oil cloth and stuff put down on the floors. I went to two primary schools. The first one was Mitchell's Primary School. It was at the corner of Danube Street and Tennent Street and it was connected to a church. I think I was there for two or three years and then I moved across to a school called Edenbrook and that was actually in Tennent Street as well. I moved on to Summerdale Secondary School which would have been on the Upper Crumlin Road.

Ann Henry – 29

I was born in the Shankill in Tenth Street, that was just off the Shankill. There was Tenth Street, Ninth, Eighth, Seventh, Sixth, and it went right down to First Street. I was born in 1955 in a two up and two down house. My parents were Billy and Isobel Grant and both my parents always worked. My Daddy worked in the shipyard I think from he was 14, he never ever had any other job, and my mummy always worked too. She worked in the Tilley Lamp and she worked in The Standard, and I remember she used to leave the house very early in the mornings because she had to get a blue bus.

Bill Henry – 26

I was born on the 9th of February 1954, in a place called Keswick Street. It's just off Tennent Street there facing the police station. I was actually born in the house. It used to be then that your neighbours would have come in and delivered the babies around the streets. It was a Mrs Tumalty that lived next door to me who delivered me, and I wouldn't cry and I'd no voice, and she put me under the water tap and that's how I got the voice. And the wife says, every now and again, 'I wish she hadn't have put you under the water tap', because I never shut up now.

Jackie Henry – 9, 23

I was born in 1948 in 47 Commedagh Drive, Andersonstown. I have three brothers and one sister. I was reared there until I was eight years old. I went to a Protestant school on the Falls Road called Roselawn. My mother, Violet Henry, was from Montreal Street, Oregon Street, at the top of the Shankill. My father Edward Henry, Ned Henry as he got, was from Cupar Street. My father was a labourer. He actually worked for the electricity board, putting up all the lighting throughout the country. My mother and father had it very hard. It was from pillar to post. My mum used to get stuff in the Co quarter and there was 13 weeks to pay it back and everything went into Walters's pawn shop in Leopold Street. It was all pawned to get money to feed us for that 13 weeks and it was never redeemed. Then you had the wee tick man who used to come.

Ruby Hill – 51, 57

I was born in 1938. I lived in Memel Street, off East Belfast. I had two older sisters. And I have one sister younger than me. My sister wasn't well, she had TB, so we had to move house because the doctor had prescribed her to get clean air as we were in amongst the buildings at the shipyard and all. We went to West Circular Road first, and then to the Grosvenor Rd and we lived there for about 7 or 8 years. One side of the Grosvenor Road was Catholic and the other side was Protestant, but I think I was on the Catholic side more times because I was at an age when I was going about with friends. At that time there was no trouble. Everybody was living together and quite content and happy to do that. Then we moved down into Ballybeen, and I've been living there ever since.

Norman Hunt – 20
I was born in 1951 in Pernau Street which was off Carlin Street in the upper Shankill. I was the second one of my family and I have six sisters. There were seven children, two adults and an aunt, and we lived in two bedrooms. Life was pretty rough. We hadn't too much. You had to be the first one downstairs in the morning to get a round of bread. You toasted it in front of the fire with an old fork and the other ones came down and you couldn't get round the fire. My father was a house repairer. He got work off people who needed walls plastered, or ceilings put up. From I was about 8 year old I was helping him to mix sand and cement.

Billy Hutchinson – 117
I was born on the Shankill in 1955 and I grew up in a two up two down house. My father had grown up in Conway Street. He worked for bookmakers. At that time it was mostly Catholics that worked in the bookies. My mother worked on the Antrim Road and cleaned houses belonging to the Jewish community. Both of them worked hard. There was me, my sister and my brother. I was the youngest. A couple of days a week if she hadn't been working my mother would have taken me to the Shankill library and sat me down in front of the books. She was a great reader, she'd have read a book a day if she'd have got the chance. My mother came from a very strong unionist family, and my father I suppose in many ways was a socialist. All his friends were Catholic, because of where he came from, at the lower end of Conway Street. I always say I grew up in a sort of mixed marriage because one was a unionist and one was a socialist.

Drew Johnston – 40
I was born in October 1950 in Riga Street, a street off the Shankill Road. I had two sisters, my eldest sister was Agnes who was born in 1938, and my little sister was called Mary and she was born in August 1945. I came along in 1950. There was three of us in the family. My father was born in Northumberland Street in December 1915 and moved to Riga Street in 1916. His father died when he was only 3 months old. He was a joiner in Andrews Flour Mill so they needed the house for someone to replace him. So my grandmother ended up living in Riga Street. And that's how I was born in Riga Street, because my grandmother moved in with her daughter to Riga Street and gave my mother and father the house when they were married, because houses at those times were very scarce. And my mother and father made a home of it. And I lived there until 1983, till the redevelopment.

Joan Johnston – 55
I was born in Third Street, Belfast, in 1954. It was off Conway Street and it was actually nearer the Falls than what it would be to the Shankill. It was only a one sided street because there was

a big factory - Wellman Smiths Factory. I have five sisters and three brothers, and we all lived in a three bed roomed house in Third Street. My grandmother lived with us, she was widowed at 19. My mammy worked in the mill, Greeves' Mill, and my daddy worked in the ship yard.

Jake Kane – 65
I was actually supposed to be born in Belfast but I happened to pop out over in England, in Leeds. It was because my father went over to England for a bit of work, demolition work, and I actually was born over there and brought back to Belfast. When we came over from England I lived with my grandfather for a short period of time, in the old Hopewell Street, which would be in the lower part of the Shankill, and then we moved up into James Street and we had a two up-two down house with an outside toilet at those times. I was ten years old at the outbreak of the Troubles in 1969.

Mary Kelly – 41
I was born in 1947 in Etna Drive in Ardoyne. My parents were Bridget and Joseph McLarnon. They had nine children. I was the seventh and I was the only girl. My mother was a stitcher and my father worked as an inspector for the corporation. I went to the Holy Cross Primary School in Butler Street and then moved to Holy Cross School in Chief Street. I left school and went straight into work at Grangers Shirt Factory in Ligoneil. I married John Kelly in 1968.

Ally Kennedy – 48, 77
I was born in Whitehill in Bangor. We actually lived in Omagh, down in Drumquin, for about 4 years and then came up in 1972 when I was seven. I started primary school in Kilcooley in Bangor. We were living in Loughview Terrace, down in Drumquin. It was the time that Bloody Sunday happened and I can remember all these people putting black flags out, and I wondered what the black flags were about. I remember running into my Mummy saying, 'Where is my black flag?' I didn't understand at the time. So they must have found out through the flags, because we didn't have one up, and they actually put us out of that area. When we were out they burned the house. We didn't have any stuff in it but they burned the house. It must have been to make sure that we wouldn't move back into it again. So we came back up to Bangor and it was the UDA who squatted us into Kilcooley and we have been there since.

Eddie Kinner – 61, 67
I was born in 1957 in Greenland Street, which is in Peter's Hill rather than the lower Shankill. I grew up in Christopher Street and I went to Brown Square Primary School. My dad was a labourer. He had served in the RAF but when he finished his time here he didn't have a trade so he wasn't in regular employment. So there were times when he would have been unemployed and I would have got the free dinners at school. Getting a blue dinner ticket was a form of stigma. I grew up feeling that I was in some way inferior to those who were paying for their lunch rather than getting free dinners. There was six of us, and my mother stitched hankies at home while she looked after us in order to put food on the table. It was certainly no easy life.

Andrew Larmour – 107
I was born 29th of April 1972 in the Ballybeen

estate, and grew up in Ballybeen estate all my life. Ballybeen was a great working class, loyalist community. Everybody got on with everybody. You could go running in and out of people's houses. For such a big estate, you knew everybody that lived in the estate. And I grew up, a happy family life with my mother and father and my brother.

Raymond Laverty – 118

I grew up right on the interface in east Belfast, although when I was growing up in the 60's it wasn't really an interface because there were Catholics living at the top end of our street. I suppose I'd grown up with a normal life until around about 1969 when, as a 9 year old, I knew that something was changing. My father was a footballer. He played Irish league football and he was offered a chance to go across the water to play over there. He would have gone but my mother wouldn't go. She was a home bird.

Lee Lavis – 105, 109

I was born in 1971 in Burton-upon-Trent. That's just to the south of Derby. I have a brother and a sister. I'm the eldest. We had a very working class sort of upbringing. My father was a soldier himself and later became a lorry driver for a local brewery – Burton-on-Trent is famous for producing beer – and my mother is a cleaner. I went to school in a place called Barton-under-Needwood, which is an area off Burton-on-Trent where I actually lived. The village was very wealthy, with one road of social housing. When I say wealthy, there was a guy who owned Grand National winning horses and that kind of thing. Derby County's football manager also lived in the village. So you had a lot of money in the village but you had this one road of social housing that had been built in the 1950s. I lived in the social housing.

Joan Linhart – 42

I come from Jersey in the Channel Islands, and I was born in St. Helier which is the capital, in 1929. There was just my brother and myself and my Mum. My mother and my father were, sadly, separated, but my mother was a worker and was able to start a small guest house because Jersey attracted a lot of visitors. But, of course, once the Germans came to the island we were cut off completely. They came in early July, 1940, and well, I don't know if you'd say they left, because they didn't. It was because the war was won by the allied forces and they had to surrender the islands in 1945. Everything was rationed, everything. We got no eggs at all, our ration of butter was two ounces, there was no flour, we drank what they called tea but it was only a substitute. Red Cross parcels were the first parcels that ever reached the island and believe me, we were very, very hungry. Everything with nourishment in it was in those parcels and they were beautiful. You know, tins of spam, sardines, a packet of raisins. There was powdered egg and Quaker Oats and chocolate. They were beautiful packages, beautiful.

Minnie Long – 1

I was born in 23 Saunders Street in 1919. My father was in the army and my mother had a wee shop. I don't remember it but she always told us about it. And then we moved to Moore Street on the Woodstock Road. There was six of us, three brothers and three sisters and we went to Moore Street school.

Terry Lyons – 94

I was born in our family home in Iveagh in 1946. I was the baby of the family with three older sisters, I was spoilt! My mother came from Albert Street, she was an embroidery machinist. My father came from Enniskillen, Co Fermanagh. He worked for the General Post Office. He started off as a telegram boy and came to Belfast and became the longest serving imperial post service employee. He got a commendation from London for it. He had lodgings above McKeown's forge in Eliza Street in the Markets area.

Caoimhín Mac Mathúna – 52

Rugadh mise i Londain in 1958. Phós m'athair agus mo mháthair, d'imigh siad go Londain ar mhí na meala, d'fhán siad ansin agus chaith siad thart fá dhá bhliain ansin, agus sin an áit ar rugadh mé. I ndiaidh domhsa bheith dhá bhliain d'aois, fuair m'athair post i mBéal Feirste le hoifig an phoist agus bhog muid ar ais arís.

I was born in London in 1958. My father and mother married, they went to London for the honeymoon, they stayed there and spent around two years over there, and that's where I was born. After I turned two years old, my father got a job in Belfast with the post office and we moved back.

Marcas Mac Ruairí – 116

Rugadh mé sa bhliain 1963 amuigh faoin tuath. Is dócha ag an am sin, nach gach duine a rugadh san otharlann agus rugadh mé sa bhaile i gceantar darbh ainm Ráth Cholpa, baile fearainn é ina aice le Sabhall i gContae an Dúin. Ní raibh áiseanna ar chóir ar bith ann. Bhí séipéal ann, bhí teach tábhairne ann agus bhí siopa ag m'athair ann agus sin amháin a bhí ann. Taobh amuigh de sin, bhí páirceanna ann agus bhí, mar a bheir siad air sa Bhéarla, labourers' cottages. Ní raibh mórán de shaibhreas sa cheantar. Ní raibh mé i mo chónaí ansin i bhfad. Tá cuimhní maithe agam ón áit ach bhogamar isteach i nDún Pádraig nuair a bhí mé trí bliana d'aois. Is cuimhin liom an lá gur bhogamar isteach. Ní raibh soilse tráchta ar bith i nDún Phádraig ag an am, is dócha go raibh bochtanas go leor sa bhaile agus bhí roinnt de na leaids nach raibh jabanna acu; bhí fadhbanna ólacháin acu. Is cuimhin liom ag tiomáint isteach i nDún Pádraig agus bhí beirt ólta ag troid i lár na príomhshráide agus píosa mór adhmaid ag duine amháin acu. Bhuail sé an duine éigin eile thar an aghaidh agus thosaigh an fhuil agus na fiacla ag titim amach. Sin mé ag bogadh isteach go Dún Pádraig agus mé trí bliain d'aois.

I was born in 1963 out in the country. Probably at that time, not everyone was born in the hospital and I was born at home in an area called Raholp, a townland near Saul in County Down. There were no facilities at all. There was a chapel, there was a pub and my father had a shop and that's all there was. Aside from that, there were fields and what they called 'labourers' cottages' in English. There wasn't much wealth in the area. I didn't live there for long. I have good memories of the place but we moved into Downpatrick when I was three years old. I remember the day we moved in. There were no traffic lights in Downpatrick at the time, there was probably a fair bit of poverty in the town and a lot of the lads didn't have jobs; they had drinking problems. I remember driving into Downpatrick and there were two drunk men fighting in the middle of the main street and one of them had a large piece of wood. He hit the other person over the face and blood and teeth started falling out. That was me moving into Downpatrick when I was three.

Séamus Mac Seáin – 103
Rugadh mise dhá lá i ndiaidh na Nollag, sin an seachtú lá is fiche de mhí na Nollag, naoi déag tríocha is a seacht. Tháinig mé ar an tsaol ag 29 Rodney Parade, sin taobh le Cluain an Bhogaigh, in Iarthar Bhéal Feirste. Ní raibh an mótarbhealach ann agus shínigh Cluain an Bhogaigh anonn go dtí an taobh eile den abhainn atá ansin go fóill ach go bhfuil sé clúdaithe isteach agus nach léir duit go bhfuil sé ann, go dtí go mbíonn taoide ann agus ansin cuireann sé thar bruach amach agus bíonn taoide ann dá bharr. Riasc mór a bhí ann agus shín sé chomh fada uait agus a thiocfadh leat a fheiceáil. Ba é sin an láthair shúgartha a bhí againn agus muid ag fás aníos. Bhí deichniúr sa teach ar fad. D'oibrigh m'athair Ar Iarnród Thuaisceart na hÉireann. Fear tine a bhí ann, fear guail. Mo mháthair, bhuel, le hochtar páistí, post lánaimseartha a bhí ann!

I was born two days after Christmas, the twenty-seventh of December, 1937. I was born at 29 Rodney Drive, beside the Bog Meadow, in west Belfast. The motorway wasn't there at that time and the Bog Meadows stretched out over to the other side of the river, which still exists, but which is covered now and obviously no longer there, until it floods and the banks burst and the river overflows. The whole thing was a huge marsh which stretched as far as the eye could see. That was our playground when we were growing up. There were ten in our house in all. My father worked for Northern Ireland Railways. He was a fire man, a coal man. My mother, well, with eight kids that was a full-time job!

Seán Mac Seáin – 27
Rugadh mé ar an 5ú lá de mhí Feabhra, 1943 agus as ceantar Naomh Séamais, ar Bhóthar Dhún na nGall - sin an áit ar rugadh agus ar tógadh mé. Ceantar lucht oibre a bhí ann, ganntanas airgid agus ganntanas oibre.

I was born on the 5th of February, 1943 in the St James' area, on the Donegall Road – that's where I was born and raised. It was a working class area, there was a lack of money and a lack of jobs.

Jake Mac Siacais – 73
Bhuel rugadh mise i 1958 in Ard Eoin, in Otharlann an Mater. Bhí cónaí ag mo thuismitheoirí ag an am le athair m'athara. Mise an tríú duine sa teaghlach, sa deireadh ar fad bhí naonúr. Fuair siad teach bliain ina dhiaidh sin agus fágadh mise leis an tseanlánúin. Bhog mo thuismitheoirí go Baile Andarsan, amuigh fán tuath, nó bhí ag an am. Bhí sin coitianta go leor. D'fhan mé ansin go dtí go bhfuair mo chéad seanmháthair bás, i 1963, agus bhog mé thart chuig mo gharthuismitheoirí eile i Northwich Drive; sin athair agus máthair mo mháthara. Fán am a raibh siad ag iarraidh mé a thabhairt abhaile ní raibh fonn orm gabháil!

Well I was born in 1958 in Ardoyne, in the Mater Hospital. My parents were living with my paternal grandfather at the time. I was the third child in the family, eventually there were nine of us. They got a house the following year and I was left with the old couple. My parents moved to Andersonstown, out in the country, or it was at the time. That was common enough. I stayed there until my first grandmother died, in 1963, and I moved round to my other grandparents in Northwick Drive, my mother's father and mother that is. By the time they wanted to take me home I didn't want to go!

Seán Mac Aindreasa – 14
Rugadh mé i 1940 i gceantar darbh ainm The Pound Loney. Níl an ceantar sin ann níos mó ach tá sé san áit a bhfuil tithe Dhubhaise ann anois. Bhí mo thuismitheoirí agus seachtar againn sa teaghlach. An ceantar a dtugann siad an Loney air, bhí sé iontach beag. Dá rachfá síos Sráid Albert, bhí sé idir Sráid Albert agus sráid darbh ainm Pound Street, nach bhfuil ann anois. Sin an áit a bhfuil teach an phobail Naomh Peadar anois. Bhí thart fá thrí shráid déag sa cheantar sin uilig. Agus ba é Bóthar Culantree is mó a bhí ag rith fríd an áit agus bheadh na sráideanna beaga uilig ag imeacht uaidh sin. Bhí tithe tábhairne ar beagnach gach sráid. Iontach go leor anois bhí beirt fhidléirí ina gcónaí sa tsráid s'againne, fidléirí traidisiúnta. Ach ní chluinfeá iad sna tithe tábhairne nó rud ar bith. Bheadh siad ag seinm ag na feiseanna agus bhí siad ag seinm corruair ar raidió, ar an BBC. De ghnáth ní thugann an BBC aird ar bith ar cheol traidisiúnta ar chor ar bith. Nó ar chluichí Gaelacha nó ar an teanga Ghaelach nó rud ar bith ach bhí corruair sa bhliain gheofá ceithre uair a' cloig d'fhidléir traidisiúnta éigin ar an raidió agus ar ndóighe ní raibh aon teilifís ann an t-am sin ar chor ar bith.

I was born in 1940 in an area called the Pound Loney. That area doesn't exist anymore but it's where the Divis houses are now. There were my parents and seven of us in the family. The area they called the Loney, it was very small. If you went down Albert Street, it was between Albert Street and a street called Pound Street, which isn't there now. That's where St Peter's church is now. There were around thirteen streets in that whole area. Cullingtree Road was the main one running through the area and all the little streets would come off that. There were pubs on almost every street. Amazingly enough now there were two fiddlers living in our street, traditional fiddlers. But you wouldn't hear them in the bars or anywhere. They would play at the feiseanna and they played on the radio occasionally, on the BBC. Usually the BBC doesn't pay any attention at all to traditional music. Or to Gaelic games or to the Irish language or anything but now and again during the year you'd get four hours of some traditional fiddler on the radio and of course at that time there were no TVs at all.

Seán Mag Uidhir – 66, 75
Rugadh mé i '57. Bhí mo thuismitheoirí sa cheantar sin in aice le Greenway's, ar Bhóthar Stewartstown ansin. Bhí deartháir mo mháthar ina chonaí ansin lena bhean agus rugadh mé agus iníon s'acu ar an lá chéanna. Caithfidh go raibh fleadh maith acu roinnt mí roimhe sin! Tar éis theacht ann domh, bhog siad ar ais go Béal Feirste, chuaigh siad chuig Alliance Avenue díreach in aice le Ard Eoin ansin. Bhí tuismitheoirí s'acu díreach in aice leo i sráid darbh ainm Etna Drive i nArd Eoin féin. Cé go raibh mo mháthair ón Chrois Ghearr i gContae an Dúin ó dhúchas agus Dún Phádraig. Ach,

bhog siadsan go dtí Ard Eoin sna 30í. Bhí m'thair ag obair mar bhainisteoir ar theach tábhairne, ba é sin ceann de na ceardanna a bhí ann ag am sin. San am sin rinne siad a gcuid pórtair féin. Ba le go leor Caitlicigh tithe tábhairne, ní raibh postanna ar fáil daofa sna longcheártaí nó sna monarcha móra innealtóireachta.

> I was born in '57. My parents were in the area beside Greenway's, on the Stewartstown Road. My mother's brother lived there with his wife and their daughter and I were born on the same day. They must have had a good party a few months before that! After I was born, they moved back to Belfast they went to Alliance Avenue right beside Ardoyne. Their parents were directly in front of them in a street called Etna Drive in Ardoyne itself. Although my mother was from Crossgar in County Down originally and Downpatrick. But they moved to Ardoyne in the 30s. My father worked as a bar manager, that was one of the trades available at the time. At that time he made his own porter. Plenty of Catholics owned pubs, there were no jobs open to them in the shipyards or large engineering plants.

Seán Magaoill – 19
Rugadh mé i Sráid Seirbhíse. Servia Street. Sin thíos i bparóiste Naomh Peadar. D'fhán mé ansin go dtí go raibh trí bliana d'aois agus tháinig go Bóthar na Carraige Báine. Bhí m'athair agus mo mháthar agus naonúr páistí ann. Péintéir agus dathadóir é a bhí i mo athair, mar an gcéanna lena athair roimhe.

> I was born in Servia Street. That's down in the parish of St Peter's. I stayed there until I was three years old and then went to the Whiterock Road. There was my father and mother and nine children. My father was a painter and decorator, like his father before him.

Larry Mc Gurk – 31
Rugadh i mBéal Feirste mé ach tógadh i mBaile na Scríne mé. B'as Tuaisceart na cathrach de m'athair agus lár an bhaile de mo mháthair. Rugadh mé i 1938 agus bliain ina dhiaidh sin cuireadh tús leis an Dara Cogadh Domhanda agus de thairbhe gur Poblachtóir a bhí i m'athair, ag an am sin rugadh ar chuid mhór Poblachtóirí a bhí i mBéal Feirste ag an am. Chuir siad thart fá dhá chéad nó trí chéad acu sa phríosún ar Bhóthar Chromghlinne. Agus bhí bean i mBaile na Scríne ag an am a raibh Nóra Ní Chatháin uirthi agus bhí sí iontach mór le mo mháthair. Bhuel, nuair a tháinig tús an Chogaidh Dhomhanda, chuir siad cuireadh ar mo mháthair agus orm féin dár ndóigh, bhí mise i mo leanbh ag an am, a ghabháil go dtí Baile na Scríne.

> I was born in Belfast but raised in Ballynascreen. My father was from the north of the city and my mother was from the city centre. I was born in 1938 and the following year the Second World War began and because my father was a republican, at that time many republicans who were in Belfast at the time were seized. Around two or three hundred of them were put into the prison on the Crumlin Road. And there was a woman in Ballynascreen at the time called Nóra Ní Chatháin and she was very close to my mother. Well when the Second World War began they invited my mother and I, of course I was a baby at the time, to go to Ballynascreen.

Jim McAuley – 6, 10

I was born on the 10th of June, 1945. My full name is Jamieson, but my father had the same name, so probably to differentiate between us, I was called Jim. My mother's name was Annie and her maiden name had been Doherty and the house where actually we lived, 20 Langford Street, was the house that my mother had been born in away back years previous to that. My mother worked in Rosses Mill. She worked in the spinning part of it and she used to tell me that they used to run about in their bare feet and that sort of thing. In fact, when she started work she went in as what you called a half timer. That is, in the morning they went to school and then in the afternoon they went to work in the mill. And then they left school then when they were fourteen.

Donna McIlroy – 24, 44

I was born in 1965 in Belfast City Hospital. I am an only child. I had a neighbour on either side, two old couples, one was a wee woman called Mrs Ritchie, she was a protestant and the other one was a woman called Mrs Shannon. I can still remember Mrs Shannon to this day, a lovely woman, so she was. And I remember the time they were trying to burn the bar - there was a bar at the top of our street - and there were ones coming down from Ligoniel, apparently, and attempting to set fire to the bar. And there was a few times we had to get out in the middle of the night and go round and stay in Mrs Shannon's - I called her my granny - go round and live in her house.

Norman McMaster – 33, 53

I was born in East Belfast in 1949. There were thirteen of us, and my Ma and Da. We lived in a wee kitchen house in Moore Street, that's off the bottom of the Woodstock. The three girls got the front room. Then there was five in one bed and four in the other, and the wee young one slept with our Ma and Da. We had an aunt on that side of us, and an aunt on the other side of us, so we were all together and the neighbours were good. Everybody knew everybody in Moore Street.

Alan McVeigh – 59

I was born in 1967 in Ballybeen. I lived there most of my days until I was thirty years of age. It was a great place to grow up. There was a sense of community about the place and everybody sort of looked out for each other. One of my earliest memories would have been from about four or five years of age, heading over to West Belfast, Lenadoon. My father was a delivery driver, he had the lorry, so he went over and collected everybody's furniture, brought them back over, and they were re-housed in Ballybeen. So from that age I knew that there was something going on outside in the bigger world.

Brighid Mhic Sheáin – 4

Rugadh mé i 1938 sa teach ar Shráid Derby. Rugadh achan duine sa teach ag an am sin ar ndóighe, seachas taismí. Tháinig mo mhuintir uilig ón áit ar thug siad an Pound Loney air. Ceantar na mbocht a bhí ann, ach bíonn fiú gradamach ag na boicht. Mo sheanathair, sin athair mo mháthar, French polisher a bhí ann agus cuid mhaith de na daoine faoin Pound is labourers a bheadh iontu. Chuaigh seisean suas an dréimire rud beag agus bhog siad cúpla áit agus chríochnaigh siad i Sráid Derby.

I dtéarmaí an cheantair sin, bhí sin rud beag níos airde go sóisialta.

I was born in 1938 in the house in Derby Street. Everyone was born at home at that time of course, except for accidents. All of my family came from the area called the Pound Loney. It was a poor area, but even the poor have self-respect. My grandfather, my mother's father that is, he was a French polisher and a lot of the people around the Pound would have been labourers. He got up the ladder a little bit and they moved a few places and they ended up in Derby Street. In terms of that area, that was a little higher socially.

Máire Mhic Sheáin – 16
Rugadh mé i mí Iúil sa bhliain 1940 agus tógadh mé ar Bóthar na bhFál, in aice le Teach an Phobail Naomh Peadar, ar Shráid Milford, i dteach beag sraithe. Ní raibh ann ach seomra amháin chun tosaigh agus seomra beag ar chúl agus rud ar thug muid an scullery air. Bhí an leithreas amuigh ar chúl, ní raibh seomra folctha againn agus ní raibh gairdín againn. Tháinig an fear thart uair a amháin sa tseachtain ag bailiú chíos an tí agus bhí sé iontach tábhachtach go raibh an cíos tí agat nuair a tháinig sé thart, seo daoine a chónaigh b'fhéidir i dtithe níos mó b'fhéidir suas an bóthar. Bhí meascán d'obair ag na daoine. Bhí duine thuas an tsráid, bhí athair s'acu siúd ina bread server. Ní raibh mórán mná amuigh ag obair. Ach má bhí, bhí siad ag obair sna rud ar thug muid na wear rooms orthu. Sin an áit a ndearnadh éadaí. Nó b'fhéidir go raibh siad ag obair i gcaifé.

I was born in the July of 1940 and raised on the Falls Road, beside St Peter's church, in Milford Street, in a small terraced house. There was only one front room and a small room at the back and what we called the scullery. The toilet was out the back, we didn't have a bathroom and we didn't have a garden. The man came around once a week collecting the rent and it was very important that you had the house rent when he came, these were people who perhaps lived in bigger houses up the road. People had a mixture of jobs. Someone up the street, their father was a bread server. There weren't many women out working. But if they were, they worked in what we called the 'wear rooms'. That's where clothes were made. Or maybe they worked in a café.

Caitlín Mhistéil – 11
Rugadh mé i mBéal Feirste in áit darbh ainm Rodney Parade, Bóthar Dhún na nGall ar an ochtú lá is fiche de Mí Eanáir, 1940. Chaith mé an chéad chúpla bliain de mo shaol in áit darbh ainm Laurencetown de thairbhe go dtáinig an cogadh. Bhí m'athair ag obair ar an bhóthar iarainn, an GNR, ag an phointe sin dena shaol agus bheadh seisean ag taistil ó theach s'againne in Rodney go dtí Laurencetown.

I was born in Belfast in a place called Rodney Parade, Donegall Road on the twenty-eighth of January, 1940. I spent the first few years of my life in a place called Laurencetown because the war came. My father worked on the railways, the GNR, at that point in his life and he would travel from our house in Rodney to Laurencetown.

Hugh Mornin – 21, 46
I was born down the Newtownards Road, a

place called Solway Street, in 1946, a long time ago. The Newtownards Road was very much different in them days. I was the baby in the family and there was my mum and my dad, my brother and my sister, myself and my uncle, my mother's brother, all lived in the same house. It was a two bed-roomed house. The first five years of my life my father didn't have any sort of steady employment. He came back after the war and at that time unemployment was high. And he might have got a job for a day or two and then laid off again. So this happened until I was about five-years-old and then he got work in the tabulating factory on the Castlereagh Road. Everybody called it the Tab. There was never much money about but we never felt poor. Everybody was in the same boat.

Betty Morrison – 43, 91

I was born on the 18th of February, 1952, in the Royal Victoria Hospital. We lived in Bellevue Street up the Shankill Road. I have one younger brother. There's six years between him and me. Mum and Dad always worked, so they did, were never out of work. One thing to the other, just getting on, day by day, the way it was back in them days. My dad used to be on the trams and he drove the lorries for Wordies, and my mum worked in Ewarts Mill on the Crumlin.

Paddy Mulvenna – 92

I was born in 1929 in the Oldpark, the Sacred Heart district, called the Bone. There were seven of us in the family, four boys and three girls. My mother was a mill worker from Belfast and my father came from the Glens of Antrim.

William Mitchell – 74

I was born in the City hospital in Belfast in 1958. I near said 56 there for some reason. In 1958. All my early childhood I grew up in the area around York Street known as the Docklands. My father was from Cosgraves Street in Tigers Bay, and my mother was from Little York Street. The two of them met socialising in and around those areas which at that time were full of dancehalls and the bars. My mum was a bit of a nomad and we moved lots of times in those small terraced houses between Tigers Bay and York Street. In those days the granny was the glue that seemed to tie families together. My granny lived in a house in Little York Street and our primary school was off York Street. So after school we went to our granny's house which was only across the street. So me and my sister ended up practically living there. Later on we went to Rathcoole where my kid brother was born when I was fourteen.

Jim Neeson – 98

I was born in 1940 in Scotland. My father left Ireland in 1937 and found work on the railways in Lanarkshire and that was how he met and fell in love with my mother Sarah McIlhenny. She was from the Gorbals the notorious ghetto of poverty in Glasgow. My mother died of peritonitis 6 weeks after my birth. There were two of us and we were then brought up by my great aunt and uncle Cassie and Paddy Dean. I was reared in Newington for five years until I started school and went to school in the Holy Family. After a short period in St. Malachy's I left school. My family were involved in transport and lorries and driving was all I was interested in.

Robert Niblock – 115

I was born in 1955 in a small area in East Belfast called Lagan Village. It's like a triangle between the Old Woodstock Road, Ravenhill Road, and My Lady's Road. I have two sisters, one younger and one older, and two years between each of us. I was born in a street called Swift Street. My mother came from a large family in the same area. Her maiden name was Bennett and they were a big family. At that stage, in the 50s and 60s, they would have been seen as one of the leading Unionist or Loyalist families. They were in bands, they were in the Orange, the Black, the Apprentice Boys. They were in Rangers' clubs, they were in Linfield Supporters' Clubs. My father's family came from the next street, a street called Rathmore Street. My father came from a family which had sort of two sides. His mother married twice and he had step brothers and sisters, and they were also a mixed family, my grandmother's previous marriage was to someone from the Falls Road. I was very, very close to my mother's side of the family and not so close to my father's side of the family.

Gearóid Ó Cairealláin – 62

Rugadh mise sa bhliain 1957, mar sin tá mé sé bliana is caoga d'aois faoi láthair. Rugadh mise in Iarthar Bhéal Feirste agus tógadh mé in Iarthar Bhéal Feirste, chónaigh mé mo shaol uilig in Iarthar Bhéal Feirste.

> I was born in 1957, so I am currently 56 years old. I was born in west Belfast and raised in west Belfast, I have lived my entire life in west Belfast.

Peadar Ó Cuinneagáin – 35

Rugadh mé i 1960, Bealtaine, agus tógadh mé i Sráid Clyde, ar Bhaile Mhic Gearóid, nó an Trá Ghearr, mar a bheirtear air. Mo mháthair, m'uncail agus m'aintíní, thugaidís Baile Mhic Gearóid air. Mé féin agus glúin s'againne, an Trá Ghearr; 'The Short Strand' sula raibh an Ghaeilge againn.

> I was born in 1960, in May, and I was raised in Clyde Street, in Ballymacarret, or the Short Strand as it's called. My mother, my uncles and aunts, they would all call it Ballymacarret. Myself and my generation, An Trá Ghearr, or The Short Strand before we could speak Irish.

Liam Ó Maolchloiche – 30

Rugadh mé i 1956, ar an 9ú lá de mhí na Samhna. Oíche Aoine a bhí ann, agus rugadh mé sa teach ina bhfuil mise i mo chónaí go fóill, cé go raibh mé ar rotha mór an tsaoil cúpla uair, tá mise ar ais arís. Dúradh liom go raibh fleadh ann sa chistin a fhad is a bhí mo mháthair ag tabhairt breithe domhsa! Rugadh mé ag cúig chun a hocht. Mise an chéad mhac a bhí ag m'athair agus mo mháthair, bhí ceathrar iníonacha acu, Betty, Carol, Marie agus Vera. Tháinig comharsan dár gcuid, fear darbh ainm Jimmy Parker, agus chuir sé Guinness thar mo chloigeann mar bhaisteadh. Bhaist sé mé le Guinness, an chéad mhac a bhí ag Annie agus Billy Stone. Ní raibh dúil agam sa bheoir ó shin!

> I was born in 1956, on the ninth of November. It was a Friday night, and I was born in the house in which I still live, although I was out on the hard road a few times, I'm back again. I was told that there was a fleadh in the kitchen while my mother was giving birth

to me! I was born at five to eight. I was the first son my mother and father had, they had four daughters – Betty, Carol, Marie and Vera. A neighbour of ours, a man called Jimmy Parker, came and put Guinness on my head as a baptism. He baptised me with Guinness, the first son of Annie and Billy Stone. I had no interest in the drink ever since!

Pilib Ó Ruanaí – 50
Rugadh agus tógadh mé i mBaile Mhic Airt, an Trá Ghearr, 1959. Tá mé ceithre bliana agus caoga anois. Mise an deichiú páiste as clann de thrí dhuine dhéag. Rugadh agus tógadh mé i Sráid Andarsan ar an Trá Ghearr. Tá pobal de thrí mhíle daoine anois ann in oirthear Bhéal Feirste. An t-aon cheantar náisiúnach in oirthear Bhéal Feirste i gContae an Dúin, ar an taobh eile den abhainn Lagáin. Bhí fostaíocht ann i ndiaidh an chogaidh agus le linn an chogaidh bhí roinnt Caitliceach ag obair ansin. Is dóigh liom, sna seascaidí ní raibh cúrsaí chomh dona sin. Bhí Richardson's Fertilisers ar an Trá Ghearr féin agus bhí go leor daoine sa cheantar fostaithe ansin agus bhí an áit sin foscailte go dtí, b'fhéidir cúig bliana déag ó shin, nuair a druideadh é. Sílim go raibh sé faoi úinéireacht Rialtas na Sé Chontae is Fiche ag an am sin, nuair a druideadh sin. Bhí an Sirocco Works ann go díreach i lár báire, bhí muid cóngarach le clós na loinge. Is dóigh liom go raibh cúpla míle duine fostaithe ann. Ní shílim go raibh duine ar bith, ar feadh m'eolais, a bhí fostaithe ann arbh as an Trá Ghearr iad. Ba ghnách linn na daoine sin a fheiceáil ag siúl suas agus anuas an bóthar ag am lóin nó i ndiaidh a gcuid oibre ag dul abhaile go dtí Newtownards Road nó Castlereagh Road nó cibé áit. Níor shíl daoine mórán de, níor chuir siad suntas ann nach raibh duine ar bith sa cheantar fostaithe ann.

I was born and raised in Ballymacarret, the Short Strand, in 1959. I'm fifty-four years old now. I was the tenth child in a family of thirteen. I was born and raised in Anderson Street in Short Strand. There's now a community of three thousand people there in east Belfast. It's the only nationalist community in east Belfast in County Down, on the other side of the River Lagan. There was employment after the war and during the war there were a number of Catholics working then. I suppose that in the Sixties that things weren't so bad. Richardson's Fertilisers was in Short Strand itself and plenty of people from the area were employed there and that place was open until maybe fifteen years ago, when it was closed. The Sirocco Works were central and we were close to the shipyard. I think there were a few thousand people employed there. I don't think there was anyone, as far as I know, employed there from Short Strand. We used to see those people walk up and down the road at lunchtime or after work going home to the Newtownards Road or Castlereagh Road or wherever. People didn't think much of it, they didn't pay much attention to the fact nobody from the area was employed there.

Stevie O Reilly – 96
I was born in 1973 in Belfast. My mother's name is Mary Hannon and she is originally from Ballymurphy. My father's name is Liam O Reilly and he is from Ross Road in Belfast. He is a furnace operator. I have two sisters. I went to St Gall's Primary School and then to the Christian Brothers' School on the Glen Road.

May Paul – 63

I was born in 1932 and I was brought up on the Shankill and I was one of 9 children. There was five more but they died as wee babies. But when the war broke out we were evacuated to Ballymoney. There was my Mum and just us seven kids at that time. And when we got to Ballymoney they couldn't get a place for the seven of us. They put us into the Root Hospital in Ballymoney and they were going to split us up, but Mum said that she wouldn't part with any of us. We were there nearly a week and she sent my Dad a letter to come and bring us home for she had no money or nothing. Just as that happened somebody came into the Root Hospital, to the staff, and said that they'd found her a cottage. And it was wonderful. We stayed there, I think, three years. We had a lovely time. I'll never forget the experience of living in the country. There was no rationing. You got eggs everyday off the farmer. He was in charge of us, but he was a good landlord. Eggs and milk and butter, it was all free, so my Mum baked all her own bread. It was a wonderful time for her too for she got peace to live.

Michael Pike – 79

I was born 54 years ago in Douglaston Stables, Milngavie, which is a place just outside Glasgow. I have two older sisters, Evelyn and Denise, and a younger sister, Christine, she's only 18 months younger than me. And my younger brother Derek who came six years after I was born. So there were five of us. My mum was originally from Glasgow. She was from Yoker. My mum is an incredibly strong woman. She was a grafter, a feminist, and she cleaned bars and was a chamber maid. When she got to the age of forty she was, 'ah I'm fed up cleaning out men's toilets. I'm better than this.' So she became a nurse at the age of forty. My father is English and he comes from a large family in Quorn in Leicestershire. My dad was from mining stock. His father died when he was six years old of coal dust on the lungs. He was in the navy when he met my mother; he was based up in Rothesay. And he met my mum and they quickly got married and he stayed in Scotland since. So he put up with a fair bit of racial abuse, being English, when being English in Glasgow was not the best thing to be in the 50's and 60's.

Johnston Price – 102

I was born in 1954 and grew up in St. Ives Gardens on the Stranmillis Road in south Belfast. I was the first of two sons. My brother, Gerald, was born three years and eight months later. My father worked all his life in transport. My mother grew up on the Cregagh Road in East Belfast. My father actually grew up in Sandymount Street. When they got married they moved to St Ives which was literally 100 yards from where my father grew up. He didn't stray too far from the same place. It was a wonderful environment to grow up in because you just went into the street. There was always someone to play with, girls and boys. Street games, football up the top of the street. Even now I could almost name you all the families in each of the houses in the street. Even the adults were kind of familiar to you. It was a very warm place to grow up.

Alan Quail – 110

I was born in 1954. Originally we came from Jennymount Street, along York Street, York Road. Because I had pretty bad chest problems in my early years my mum got a letter from a doctor to get us out of a damp house in Kinymount Street, and we moved down to Rathcoole. It was only being built then in about '55, '56, thereabouts. It was mostly all fields. You thought you were in the countryside. Fields and trees and the glen and all, which was a cracker place to play in. There were four boys and two girls and Mum and Dad. My father had quite a few jobs. In his earlier working life he was what they called a cabinetmaker in the shipyards, woodworking and stuff. He was pretty good with his hands. That went right through to the '80s and then it sort of tapered off with the decline of the major companies, like Mackie's.

Jim Rea – 83
I was born on Bryson Street on the Newtownards Road, 1960. I can't remember the house in Bryson Street. We then moved down the Newtownards Road to Josephine Street. It was a two or three bedroom house and there were eleven of us. A couple of the older ones had moved out by the time we had moved to Tullycarnet. It was more or less because of the Troubles. The house got petrol bombed in '69, it got hit by petrol bombs but no damage was done. That night we all got moved down to St Martin's Church and locked in there because of the Troubles.

Seamus Rice – 70
I came from Edward Street, Belfast, what was known as the Half Bap, Little Italy. That's what you called the district. We then moved to the New Lodge road in the 50s. I had five sisters and three brothers. My father was a labourer with Harvey McLaughlin. My mother was a housewife, she came from Brown Street. They were all Catholic streets then.

Paul Rooney – 90
I was born in 1958 in our front room in Islandbawn Street. We were all born there except my brother, he was born in Ardboe, County Tyrone. There were five in our family, two brothers, myself, and two sisters. At an early age my mother worked in the RVH as a domestic. She came from Ardboe, but was born in the Bronx in New York. Her mother died on Christmas Eve when she was very young. She was then reared by her father, but was later sent back to Ireland to her aunt in Ardboe. My father was from the Kashmir Road and he was a bread server for Kennedy's bakery.

Sean Simpson – 34, 38
I was born in January 1959, in the Royal Maternity Hospital. There was 8 surviving children at that stage. Two had died at child birth. I was reared with 5 sisters and two brothers. A brother later got killed by the British Army in 1971. My father was a chimney sweep and he would have gone all over Belfast. My father moved on and worked in Inglis's bakery and did some part time jobs, but the majority of the time he was unemployed as was endemic probably with most men in West Belfast at the time. My mother always had wee part time jobs, usually working in shops. I was born and reared in Andersonstown. We moved into the estate when it was first developed about 60 years ago. We were the first people into the street, Glenshane Gardens. It always seemed to be filled with children and my earliest memories are of loads of children playing in the street.

Margaret Smith – 69

I was born in 1951 in a wee house in Harding Street which was off the New Lodge Road. I was the oldest. I had a brother, two years after me and then I had a sister in 1957 and then another sister in '64. She was a twin but her twin died at birth. My father was originally from the Free State and had come up to Northern Ireland to join the air force. That's how my Mammy met him. And then when he was de-mobbed he came here to try to get some work. He worked in farms and stuff up in Stormont and he went to England to work for a while and he came back and my Mammy got a wee house in Ludlow Street. It was just round the corner from Harding Street and we went to live there. Again, a kitchen house, backyard toilet, no hot water. Scullery, kitchen and two bedrooms. And then my father got a job as a telephone engineer with the GPO which is now known as BT. Mammy always worked. She was a weaver. She left school at fourteen and went straight into the factories to work. She always distinguished between factory and mill. She said she never worked in a mill. She was a weaver. She worked in a factory.

Donna Spence – 86

I was six months when I came to Tullycarnett. My mum, my dad, and my brother. My brother's physically and mentally handicapped, he's 4 ½ years older than me and there was just the two of us. Because he was the way he was I led a bit of a sheltered life. I started Tullycarnett Primary School when I was four and just played mostly with my friends in our own wee square. There was ten wee houses in our wee square. Never really got to know many more people in the estate and then the strike came. That was the first I really knew about any of the Troubles - when the strike happened.

Kay Spence – 93

I was born in 1949 in East Belfast, off Island Street, and then we moved up to the Shankill whenever I was two. I've lived on the Shankill all of my life from then. There was my Mammy, my Daddy, my granda, and six of us. My brother Billy died so that left five of us children. My Daddy was in the navy when the war was on. When he came out of the navy he got a job in Short's, and he worked there right on up until he retired at sixty five. It was rough going because my Daddy was the only one working in the house. But it was a very happy childhood. My Mammy and Daddy were very close. My Daddy sang and my Mammy played the harmonica. There was no TV, only the radio. So I was always listening to the music on the radio.

Ann Stevenson – 71

I was born on the Shankill Road in 1955. I came from a large family. If we all had survived it would have been 13 brothers, but I have 6 brothers living, myself, and my mother and father. We lived in a two-up two-down house, in Belgrave Street. From what I remember Mother was always in having kids, and because I was the only girl, I was sort of the wee mammy and had to cook and clean for them. Then you were out on the street scrubbing a big half-moon outside your door, so your mummy would notice when she got out of hospital. You learnt very quickly how to make dinners, and everything else, too. I went to a wee school at the top of our street, and then when you turned ten you moved over to Hemsworth Square, the Hen House, it got called. We spent our P6 and P7 years in there, a good wee school, and then I moved up to Everton Secondary School when I hit eleven.

Florence Stockman

I was born in 1935 and was christened Florence Page. My parents' names were Florence and David. My father was a machine man and my mother was a spinner. I had a sister who was born on the 3rd of June in 1936, but she died on the 9th of February 1938, and my mother and father separated six months later and my mother raised me on her own. I was raised with my granny Foster and my Aunt Annie and my mother in Canmore Street. I grew up with three women. I had three mothers and no father. My granny Foster came from County Fermanagh and my granda came from Sandy Row. My granny came down here to live when she got married. My granny never worked till she got married, and then she had to go to work because my granda was killed in the Battle of the Somme when my mother was only 11 months.

David Stitt – 108

I was born in 1971 in Templemore Avenue Hospital, just off Templemore Avenue in East Belfast. I lived in Saunders Street right at the bottom of the Newtownards Road for about a year, and then my mum and dad moved to Hollycroft Avenue which is off Bloomfield Avenue. One of the earliest memories I have was the police coming searching that house and land rovers being outside in the street. And then we moved to Tullycarnett, I think my Ma wanted us away from most of the trouble happening on the Newtownards Road. But we never cut our ties or links. We were always coming down the road every day. I've a younger brother, Jonathan. He's five years younger than me. My dad was a welder in the shipyard. All my dad's family worked in Harland and Wolff. They were all welders and steelworkers.

Charlie Tully – 3

I was born on the 14 April,1950, and I was born in St John's nursing home on the Crumlin Road, opposite the jail. There was a small nursing home, I think, attached to the hospital. I was then taken to Glasgow where I spent the first 10 years of my life. We lived at 174 Randolph Drive, in Clarkston. And every summer my mum would bring us - we would come home when the football season was over - and we would stay with my granny in St James' Road where we eventually came back to live when my dad finished at Celtic.

Jackie Upton – 82

I was born in a two up bedroom house in Tamar Street on the Newtownards Road. My daddy was a compositor and my mummy cleaned all her life. We lived in Tamar Street and then moved to Ribble Street and then down into Glenallen Street. I have two brothers and two sisters. I was the eldest of five. We all shared the one room until we moved into Ribble Street and we had a parlour house. So then we had an extra room, because the front room was used as a bedroom with a bed settee in it. There was no bathroom, just a tin bath, and still an outside toilet right up until 1983. We had what you called a geezer which ran on gas, and you pulled it across and it was like instant hot water through a gas system, so that was quite posh for us.

Susie Vallely – 68

I was born in Shanlieve Road in Andersonstown in 1955, I was born in the house that I lived in. I had two brothers and four sisters. I was the youngest girl. There was Geordie, then Bridget, then Margaret, Marie, then me, and then Billy. So I was the youngest girl. My mummy was from the Kashmir Road and she was Brannigan before she was married. My daddy was from Carrick Hill, Unity Street in Carrick Hill. I had just started school when my mummy died, so I was only five and Billy was only four weeks old when she died, and I have no memories of her whatsoever. People say that maybe I've blocked it because it was too painful. But my daddy was a brilliant daddy so in that sense we were very lucky. He always worked. My daddy was an asphalter so he could have been away out from half four in the morning. He worked in Portadown, Lurgan, Armagh, he worked all over. And my older sisters looked after me and Billy, my sister Marie, she was eight.

Jim Watson – 17

I was born in 1942 in the middle of the war. I was born in Montréal Street, which lies in a triangle between the Crumlin Road, the Woodvale Road and Cambria Street. You have Montréal Street, you have Oregon Street, you have Ottawa Street. You feel you're in Canada. My mother, in her early days, would have been what you call a netter in the Belfast rope works. Their whole family connection, her sisters were all there, and my elderly aunt was a forewoman in the rope works. They travelled from the Shankill Road to the rope works every day. And my father was a stager in the shipyard. My parents tell me when they got that house in Montréal Street it was just after the blitz of 1941 which badly hit our area. In fact our house was the second last house standing. On the other side of the street, half of the street at the top end and the bottom end were both blown away. So, we had, as I often said, we had a waste ground and a football pitch which the Germans gave us where they knocked down the houses. So we had plenty of room to play.

Jim Watt – 81

I grew up in Silver Stream in North Belfast. When my parents moved to Silver Stream they were just a young family and it was a brand new estate. I was only about a year old when we moved to it. So most of the people that were in the street were all young families, all growing up and that's where my childhood was. My father was a moulder in the shipyard. He had been a Dunkirk veteran of the D day landings. My mother was a housewife. And my childhood was nothing but happy. I had a brother and three sisters. I went to Carsglen Primary School. The estate I lived in was a mixed estate. We had friends, Catholic and Protestant, it didn't matter.

Jude Whyte – 22, 85

I was born in University Street in 1957. I believe I was born at home because my father, apparently, came into the bedroom and said, 'My god, that fella has a terrible big head', so it's all been downhill since then. My father was a Rasharkin man whose parents came down to settle in Belfast My mother was from the Markets, a wee place called Little May Street. My mum and dad both worked in Tourney Brothers, which is a fruit company. I think it's gone now but in those days my father was an accountant and my mother was a clerical officer. There were

10 children and two adults lived in our house which was basically a small terraced house. My mother wanted everybody to get the 11+ and get to a grammar school and that was a recurring theme in her life and in my life.

Rachel Wylie
I was born in 1947 in Ninth Street. I was the youngest of four children. I had one sister and two brothers, and everybody said we were a very close knit family. I lived with my mum and dad, and also my mum's mum, our grandmother who was even stricter than mum. But I am very proud of the mother and father and granny that I had. Our house was a very small house. There was just what you would call now a living room, and you had two bedrooms up the stairs, and you had one bedroom down the stairs. Mum worked in the mill. It was probably Ewarts Mill. There was two big mills in Belfast, one was on the Falls and one was on the Crumlin Road, so I think mum worked in the Crumlin Road one, but then she retired when the family came along. Dad was a coal man. He filled the bags and delivered the coal. He used to come home completely black. He used to have to wash himself before we sat down for a meal and in those days there was no bathrooms.

STORIES
SCÉALTA

SOLICITORS
Upper Springfield
Resource Centre
Ionad Frank Cahill

1   **A penny worth of chips**
    Minnie Long

It was Ethel McMaster that took me to get me a job in the new mill, the Jaffa Mill on the Newtownards Road. I was fourteen. Ethel and my mother were good friends. My mother worked in the mill too. She was a doffing mistress. I worked with a girl who lived in the Short Strand. You called her Mary McStravick, I remember she was the only Catholic in the spinning room. I worked in the mill from 8 o'clock in the morning, you got off an hour for your lunch. If you had a penny you bought a penny worth of chips. We had a good life.

2   **What time do the Protestants go out to play football?**
    Eileen Bell

I stayed in the country a lot because at that time, coming up to the end of the war, there was still rationing and the family thought it was better if I stayed with my granny. So when I was 5, I think it was, I started in the school down just beside the chapel, in Finnis, and that was my first experience of school. In those days, although they wouldn't have called themselves it, it was integrated. I loved it. There was a big, big old burner in the middle of the room, like Victorian times. I don't remember what I was actually taught, I have to say, but I do remember all the people with me, and I remember us sitting and talking about, 'What do you do in your church?' and no sign of anything. I was eventually in the Alliance Party, and I think I was Alliance from the day I went to that school.

When I left there and came up to Belfast it was a very dramatic change. I was about 6 or 7 when I went up to St Kevin's school which was on the Falls Road. The teacher put me beside this wee girl who lived quite near me and half way through the morning I said to her, 'What time do the Protestants go out to play football?' She looked at me and she said, 'What do you mean?' I said, 'Well, in the school that I was before, whenever we were having religious knowledge, because the Protestants had Sunday school, they went out to play football when we had our half hour or so of religious knowledge'. So she stood up, 'She went to school with Protestants', and the teacher had to rescue me, to a certain extent. Actually they looked at me as if I was an alien, but I went on to have a happy time at St Kevin's.

3   **What would this be like filled?**
    Charlie Tully

It was December 1949 at Windsor Park, Belfast Celtic against Linfield, and there are various conflicting views and opinions about what happened on the day. But the reality is that disgraceful scenes took place which should never take place at any sporting event. Players were attacked and seriously injured, in particular Jimmy Jones who had a double leg break, and apparently at one stage in the hospital they contemplated amputation. To think that this man not only got over that but came back and continued to play, and scored a total of 550 league goals which is a record to this day. What a man. He's still alive now at 84 years of age. He played on the same Belfast Celtic team as my dad, before my dad signed to Glasgow Celtic in 1948. But those disgraceful scenes happened on that day, and the Irish Football Association really didn't take any responsibility as they should have done. Celtic then went on tour to America and beat Scotland, a famous international team, and returned and the feeling is that a lot of the Belfast Celtic directors of the time didn't have the stomach to continue. I think part of the problem was that some of them were businessmen and not strictly football men. As I understand it, Elisha Scott was retained as a manager for quite a number of years when Celtic stopped playing. He went over to the park every day.

Elisha Scott, Liff Scott, was a legend at Liverpool, an international goalkeeper, a man who was very strict in his attitude to football. He was made Belfast Celtic manager, initially with the reserve team and had phenomenal success. Then he became manager of the first team. His one and only objective was to win. He didn't care who the players were, where they came from, what colour they were, what religion they were, it didn't matter. It was all about creating a football team that played and won. I have no doubt that if Belfast Celtic had stayed in Irish league football they could have been the most successful side that ever was.

Liff Scott signed my dad actually. My dad signed for Belfast Celtic on the window ledge of the Rock Bar. Belfast Celtic meant a lot to my dad. His first success in football was at Belfast Celtic. When my father had finished playing for Glasgow Celtic we were back in Belfast living in St James's Road, and every Sunday morning we went down to Celtic Park when Davy McNeill, the caretaker from Rodney, opened up, got the showers going and we played on that great ground. And I stood there as a wee boy of 13 or 14, thinking to myself, 'what would this be like filled?' I never saw it. But now there's the Belfast Celtic trail which was developed with the cooperation and financial help of the IFA.

It's basically plaques mounted at relevant places, and it's the storyline about the foundation of the club, the first clubrooms, Celtic Park, my dad's grave, and other features as you go along. So you start down at the lower Falls and you finish up on the Glen Road.

4   **Ag foghlaim na Gaeilge i mBéal Feirste sna 50í**
Brighid Mhic Sheáin

Bhí mé ag freastal ar achan rud. Bhí múinteoir i gCluain Árd, Alf Ó Murchú, agus bhí seisean iontach maith, duine ó chorrán tíre, ní raibh éirí in airde ar bith aige. Bhí sé ag iarraidh uchtach a thabhairt dúinn an t-am uilig. Agus dúirt sé, 'nuair a thosaigh mise ag foghlaim Gaeilge chuaigh mé ar 5 rang sa tseachtain'. Agus chuaigh mé abhaile agus dúirt mé, 'Right, gheobhaidh mise 5 rang sa tseachtain, rang achan oíche.' Bhuel níor éirigh liom, ach bhí cúpla ceann i gCluain Árd, bhí dhá oíche acusan, bhí ar a laghad ceann amháin san Ardscoil, agus d'aimsigh mé ceann thart i sráid bheag ar Bhóthar na bhFál. Ní raibh a fhios agam cérbh iad ar ndóighe, Craobh Saoirse na hÉireann. Sórt dream de phoblachtaigh a bhí iontu ach ní raibh a fhios agam sin. An t-aon rud a theagasc siad dúinn ná an dóigh le 'Ár n-athair' a rá i nGaeilge. Rud iontach ag dream mar sin! Chuaigh mé ar ais roinnt seachtainí ina dhiaidh sin agus bhí an áit folamh, agus shuigh mé ansin ag rá liom féin; 'Tá achan duine mall anocht'. Agus shuigh mé, agus shuigh mé, agus ansin ag an deireadh tháinig duine éigin isteach, agus dúirt mise; 'Cad é atá cearr, an bhfuil an rud ar ceal?' Agus dúirt sé; 'Aidh cinnte, tá siad uilig thuas sa Crum.' Tógadh an t-iomlán acu in midnight swoops! Chuir sin deireadh leis sin!

Learning Irish in Belfast in the 50s
Brighid Mhic Sheáin

I attended everything. There was a teacher in the Cluain Ard, Alf Ó Murchú, and he was very good, he was from the country and didn't put on any airs and graces. He was always trying to encourage us. And he said, 'When I started learning Irish I went to five classes a week.' And I went home and I said, 'Right, I'll find five classes per week, one every night.' Well I didn't succeed, but there were a couple in the Cluain Ard, they had two nights, there was at least one in the Ardscoil, and I found one round in a wee street on the Falls Road. I didn't know who they were of course, the Branch of Irish Freedom. It was a group of republicans but I didn't know that. The only thing they taught us was how to say 'Our Father' in Irish. Surprising from a crowd like that! I went back a few weeks after that and the place was empty, and I sat there saying to myself, 'Everybody's late tonight.' And I sat, and sat, and then eventually someone came in, and I said, 'What's wrong, is it cancelled?' And he said, 'It is, they're all up in the Crum.' All of them had been lifted in midnight swoops. That put an end to it!

5 **Lead lights for church windows**
Kevin Carson

My grandfather, Hugh Carson, was originally from the Market area, and he was quite famous in his own right. He worked for McManus' and different other glazing firms in Belfast, and he specialised in doing lead lights for church windows. He actually made the lead lights and installed them. I remember seeing an article in the Belfast Telegraph, a couple of years back, singing his praises, and it gave a big long list of places that he'd actually worked in, including the Guildhall in Derry, and a lot of Masonic buildings and places like that, that had lead lights. He died when I was quite young, and my grandmother Rebecca as well. They are both buried side-by-side down in Milltown, and my father and mother would have been buried in on top of them, in the same grave.

6 **On the book**
Jim McAuley

But every single day you went down to the wee shop at the corner and you got the messages on the book, you know. It was Lily Irvine's shop actually, at the corner of Mansfield Street. And I would say Lily fed and looked after quite a few people in that neighbourhood who would have went down with their book. You got it on the book, and then on Friday your mother would have went down and she'd have added it all up and paid it. Started off again the next week and that's how people lived.

7 **Recyling was nothing new to us**
Liz Groves

You collected newspapers and you collected cardboard during the summer holidays, and that was your pocket money. So recycling was nothing new to us. You also got sent to the rag store, down to Cook's Rag Store in North Queens Street. You brought wool down and they would check them to make sure you hadn't soaked them to make them heavier. Your ma and your granny took all the buttons off them, and the zips off trousers, and they were all reused. Everybody had a button box, 'Here, go to Mrs

45

Moron and see if she has a grey button'. 'Go to Mrs Baxter and see if she has a six inch zip'. Everybody recycled, it was totally amazing.

8   **Great handball players then**
Micky Gallagher

We spent our days in the street because there was no room in our house, the same as everybody else's house, and at that time families were a lot bigger than they are now so you spent your day playing outside. Handball was great. Every Saturday and Sunday you got ones coming from Fort Street and down the Falls. Handball was played at the bottom of Locan Street where we lived. There was the likes of Manual McDonald and his brother Paddy, they were fabulous players. You're talking about hundreds of people here, and handball matches played off the one wall. Unbelievable, great times, great handball players then.

9   **In my life the troubles started in 1956**
Jackie Henry

They tell me the Troubles is going on from 1969. In my life it was from 1956. We moved out of Andersonstown because of what had happened to me and the threat to my father back then. I was in the Junior Orange Order from I was seven years old, and I used to come onto the road for the 11th and 12th celebrations, and I was going along carrying the string of the banner and coming home. You didn't realise what you were doing. It was ironic because I didn't know any difference, because when the 15th of August came we used to go and steal the wood off the Orangemen from a platform at Finaghy to burn. You just went along with the flow basically. Then some older fellas, age 18 or 19, took me down over the fields and ran heckle pins from the mills up and down my arms and legs until the blood ran out of me. And then my father had been a British soldier. It wasn't that my father was a threat when we lived in Andersonstown, it was the British Army uniform. The Official IRA actually came to him and put the gun to his head and we moved after that. We did a swap with a Catholic family from Tyndale, 27 Tyndale Crescent, and they moved and we went to a flat in Tyndale Crescent.

10   **Seeing people get locked out**
Jim McAuley

I started in Ewarts in 1960 and I was there for about 9 years. It was actually the factory side I was involved in, not the mill side of it from where they made the cloth. And when I was in the office I got the opportunity of a sort of management apprentice for a lot of years - where they sent you to the Tech and you had to go back to do GCE exams. You were going there after you came out of work at night. And in Ewarts, then, you started at 8 in the morning to 6 at night, and then you worked every other Saturday morning to 12. That was just your ordinary week, I think it was about a 48 hour week you did. Then you were going to go to the night class till about ten o clock, and then going into work for 8 in the morning. It was an experience. If anybody has ever worked in the mills, especially with the Ewarts one, there was a big clock outside it and we'd have come up in the morning and you were watching for the clock going to 8 o'clock. Once that clock went to 8 o'clock, bang, you were out and they closed the gates, you were out. People would have been running to try to get through the gate before your wee man would have got it closed, and he had a wee gate boy with him, and the two of them were pushing the gate to get it to lock people out, and I could never understand. I said, 'what are they doing?' because wee women and all were having to turn round and walk away back home again because they were maybe just a minute late. But things changed then and years later, whenever labour became scarce, the gates didn't close. In fact they were actually paying workers bonuses if you could invite other people to come up to get a job. And whenever you look back on that, it was really… I always really felt bad about that. Seeing people getting locked out.

11 **Ag cur isteach na mbunchlochanna**
Caitlín Mhistéil

Oíche Mháirt bhí rang ceoil ann le Séamas Mac Diarmada nach maireann, go ndéanfá Dia a mhaith dó. Bhí ranganna oíche Luain agus oíche Déardaoin mar atá go fóill. Bheadh cumann snámha ann b'fhéidir uair amháin sa choicís. Bheadh muid amuigh ag siúl, thógfadh muid an bus b'fhéidir go dtí an stáisiún deireanach ar Bhóthar an Ghleanna agus rachadh muid amach faoin tuath agus seo mar chuid de na ranganna. Bhí Cumann Rothaíochta ann ar an Domhnach. Rachadh muid áit éigin; Brown's Bay nó thíos ag Beannchar nó thíos ag Ard Mhic Neasa agus ní raibh mise iontach maith i mbun rothaíochta, ach bhí daoine i gcónaí sásta cuidiú leat má bhí fadhb agat le rothar, agus bheadh scaifte an-deas amuigh leat tráthnóna Dé Domhnaigh agus ansin ar ais chun tí, scriosta, ach ábalta go leor gabháil amach chuig an chéilí oíche Dhomhnaigh.

Laying the foundations
Caitlín Mistéil

On a Tuesday night there was a music class with Séamas Mac Diarmada, may he rest in peace. There were classes on Monday night and Thursday night as there still are today. There was a swimming club maybe once a fortnight. We'd go out walking, we'd take the bus maybe to the last stop on the Glen Road and we'd go into the country and this was part of the classes. There was a cycling club on a Sunday. We'd go somewhere, Brown's Bay or down to Bangor or down to Holywood and I was not very good at cycling, but people were always willing to help you if you had a problem with a bike, and there was always a very nice crowd out with you on a Sunday afternoon and then back home, knackered, but able enough to go to the céilí on Sunday night.

12 **Big Blondie**
Harry Enright

In those days you sat an exam for each secondary school. I got a scholarship to St. Malachy's, a scholarship to St. Mary's and a scholarship to Harding's Street. Harding Street was over near the docks. The Christian Brothers ran it and it was a tech with a great reputation. I chose Harding because there was a boxer teaching in Harding Street and he was starting a boxing club. There wasn't a boxing club on the Falls Road at that time. The Immaculata hadn't started then. There was sort of a makeshift one at the bottom of the Whiterock but it only ran for a few weeks, and then suddenly I heard there was this school, Harding Street, and there was a boxer and that was enough for me. It was a man named Paddy O'Neill. Big Blondie they called him. He was a university boxer and he was known among the boxing crowd in Belfast. And boxing wasn't terribly popular, it was very working class, back street. But he was starting a boxing club and it was going to be called Holy Family. And I was the first Holy Family boxer in the Ulster Hall. Myself and a fella called Dicky Ferguson. Dicky was from Carrick Hill. Paddy O'Neill started the boxing club but he was my English teacher. He taught English and Geography and he insisted school was the most important. Boxing was a great pastime. And he said to me, 'you'd be very foolish to leave school and I would advise you to go on to St Mary's'. So I went from Harding Street to St Mary's Grammar School, Barrack Street. Very few did that. They usually went into jobs or trades. And then suddenly Trench House was opening and Paddy O'Neill, my mentor, was lecturing in it. And it was him said to me to come up there. Before that, if you wanted to become a teacher, you had to get a scholarship to the Catholic training college outside London. We were advised when you were in Trench House to join the Legion of Mary and help out in youth clubs for experience and all that. So I did that and I was sent down to give a hand to Immaculata boxing club. Jack McCusker was there as a trainer. Jack McCusker was a big influence in my life. He was a labourer, not clever but full of common sense. Down to earth, no pretence at all, and no time for any waffle. And then I got an offer, a visit from two men to the Immaculata one night, to restart St. Matthew's youth club in the Short Strand. And I was happy enough with Jack, but Jack said to me, 'think of the craic with your club and my club'. Little did I know that Jack would be dead within the year. He got word just when I went over to St. Matthew's that he had leukaemia, and he was such a guy. St. Matthew's was an instant success, Ulster champions, national champions. And from there I was called to be national coach, and I took Ireland's Olympic team to Tokyo in 1964 and the Commonwealth games in 1966. I was still working away as a teacher in Bearnageeha school and I stayed there until I retired.

13 **The Cardinal's box at Casement**
Micky Gallagher

My father had just taken over as grounds man at Corrigan, which was the county ground then, and my older sister Kathleen and all were doing collections to raise money for the reconstruction of Corrigan. And then that ground came up on the other side of Mooreland, so the money that was for Corrigan reconstruction bought Casement. When Casement Park was getting built I used to run from St. Paul's up to Casement Park. I knew every worker in the place. McGowan's, which was a big firm then, was doing the asphalt, and there was P&F McDonalds, all the firms. Everybody knew me, and it used to be great when you went up on a Friday because you'd have got a wing here, and a sprassey here. My father moved into Casement, and he was the first grounds man in Casement Park when it opened. The day it opened I was, as a lad at 12 and a half, sitting in the Cardinal's Box. It's called the Cardinal's Box because the Cardinal threw the ball in that day, and when he finished he came off and came up the steps, and he was brought into the square bit where the players come out underneath. It was called the

Cardinal's Box after him. I was put in there by my father who was the grounds man, saying, 'Sit you there, don't move', because he was busy and there were thousands of people there that day.

14   An t-am a thug Nioclás Tóibín cuairt ar Bhéal Feirste
Seán Mac Aindreasa

Thug Cumann Chluain Árd cuireadh do Nioclás Tóibín theacht go Béal Feirste. Tháinig Nioc Lá Fhéile Pádraig, deireadh seachtaine na Féile Pádraig '65 muna bhfuil dul amú orm. Fear láidir a bhí ann, fear measartha beag, iascaire agus feirmeoir sa gheimhreadh. An duine a bhí ina rúnaí ar Chluain Árd an t-am sin, thug siad cúpla punt domh le haire a thabhairt dó nó le béile a cheannach do Nioclás. Ach an dóigh a raibh sé, tharla go raibh a fhios agam go raibh bean i mBéal Feirste as an Rinn ó Chontae Phort Láirge agus go raibh sí sásta béile a chur ar fáil dó. An rud ab fhearr fá dtaobh de, bhí cúpla punt agam a dtiocfadh liom deoch a cheannach leis! Chuaigh muid go dtí teach tábhairne an mhaidin sin, is dócha go raibh sé thart fána dó dhéag. Ceantar bocht a bhí ann, bhí na tithe iontach beag, ní raibh tithe scartha nó rud ar bith mar sin. Ar ndóigh, ní raibh gairdíní nó a leithéid ann. Ní bheadh spás ann do ghairdíní agus bhí an clós ar chúl an tí agus an leithreas sa choirnéal dorcha. Ní raibh solas nó rud ar bith le feiceáil. Clocha a bhí ar an chuid is mó de na sráideanna.

Chuaigh muid go dtí an teach, áit darbh ainm An Seanteach a bhí ar Shráid Albert. Teach beag a bhí ann, teach tábhairne beag. Ach bhí scaifte de mhuintir na háite istigh, fir na háite istigh agus iad uilig ag ól agus spionn ar dóigh orthu. Ach ba seo an chéad uair riamh a bhí Nioc i mBéal Feirste agus níor mhian liom é a fhágáil leis féin. Ba mhian liom dul chuig an leithreas. Dúirt mé le Nioc, tá tú maith go leor i do shuí ansin agus beidh mé ar ais chomh gasta agus a thig liom. Chuaigh mé amach go dtí an leithreas. Nuair a tháinig mé isteach arís, bhí Nioc ina sheasamh i lár an urláir agus é ag gabháil cheoil, ag ceol Bold Robert Emmet. Agus chríochnaigh sé sin agus d'iarr mise air amhrán Gaeilge a rá agus dúirt sé go n-abródh sé Sliabh na mBan. Mhínigh mé don scaifte cad é an sórt amhráin a bhí i Sliabh na mBan agus gur bhain sé le hár agus léirscrios a rinneadh ar dhaoine in 1798. Dúirt mé gur seo fear, cainteoir dúchais Gaeilge i gContae Phort Láirge, agus gur seo rud a bhain le troid a tharla idir fórsaí na Sasanach agus muintir na háite, nach raibh rud ar bith acu ach píce agus sleá. Ní raibh gunnaí nó rud ar bith acu. Agus is é Sliabh na mBan, cnoc taobh amuigh de Chluain Meala i gContae Thiobraid Árann. Chan Nioclás an t-amhrán, bhí glór iontach cumhachtach ag an fhear. Ní raibh focal Gaeilge ag duine ar bith sa teach go bhfios domhsa ach chonaic mé seandaoine ansin ag caoineadh. Bhí na deora leo i ndiaidh an scéal a chluinstin. An rud a bhí ann, sa cheantar ina raibh sé bhí Jimmy Hope Club, McCracken's, Michael O'Dwyer's. Na daoine uilig a bhí bainte acu le hÉirí Amach 1798.

When Nioclás Tóibín visited Belfast
Seán Mac Aindreasa

Cumann Chluain Ard invited Nioclás Tóibín to come to Belfast. Nick came on St Patrick's Day, St Patrick's weekend of '65 if I'm not mistaken. He was a strong man, a fairly small man, a fisherman and farmer during the winter. The secretary of the Cluain Ard at the time gave me a couple of pounds to take care of him or to buy Nioclás a meal. But as it happened I knew there was a woman from An Rinn in County Waterford in Belfast and that she was willing to make him a meal. The best thing about it, I had a few pounds to buy a drink! We went to a pub that morning, it was probably around twelve o'clock. It was a poor area, the houses were very small, there were no detached houses or anything like that. Of course there were no gardens or anything of that kind. There was no space for gardens and there was a yard at the back of the house with the toilet in the dark corner. There was no light or anything with which to see. Most of the streets were stone-paved.

We went to the bar, a placed called An Seanteach that was in Albert Street. It was a small bar but there was a crowd of locals inside, local men inside and they were all drinking and in great form. But this was the first time Nick was in Belfast and I didn't want to leave him alone. I had to go to the toilet. I told Nick, 'You're okay sitting there and I'll be back as soon as I can.' I went out to the toilet. When I came back, Nick was standing in the middle of the floor singing, he was singing 'Bold Robert Emmet'. He finished that and I asked him to sing an Irish language song and he said he'd sing 'Sliabh na mBan'. I explained to the crowd what kind of song 'Sliabh na mBan' was and that it was a massacre carried out against people in 1798. I said that this was a man, a native speaker in County Waterford, and that this was about a fight between English forces and the local people, who didn't have anything except pikes and spears. They didn't have guns or anything. And Sliabh na mBan is a hill outside Clonmel in County Tipperary. Nioclás sang the song, the man had a very powerful voice. Nobody in the bar had any Irish as far as I know but I saw old men there crying. They were shedding tears after hearing the story. The thing about it was, that in that very area there was the Jemmy Hope Club, McCracken's, Michael Dwyer's. All the people who were involved in the 1798 Rebellion.

15 **Wor Jack, he left the backs all standing**
Samuel Aughey

We're a talented family. My uncle Albert is known as the Shankill poet, and there is a famous loyalist song which everybody sings now - 'A wee spot in Europe' - my mother wrote that. I remember quite some time ago going over to Glasgow a couple of time to see Rangers and there was a guy standing outside Ibrox selling wee postcard size copies of 'a wee spot in Europe'. And it was my mother wrote it. And I wrote that song 'Wor Jack'. It was about a guy Jackie Milburn who came from Newcastle and signed for Linfield. It was printed in one of the Linfield programs – 'A song written by two young Linfield supporters who are members of Oldpark Blues Supporters'. We wrote that song - 'Wor Jack, they never saw him coming, down the middle of the field, he left the backs all standing'. I've been to a few Linfield matches recently and the guys are still singing that song with a few changes to modernize it you know.

16 **...go mbeadh sin ina chuidiú ag na páistí**
Máire Mhic Sheáin

Ní rud úrnua é clann a thógáil le Gaeilge ach na daoine a rinne sin, bhí siad scaipthe fríd an chathair. Níor bhuail na páistí le chéile an méid sin agus mhothaigh siad go raibh siad ar a n-aonar. Agus cuid b'fhéidir nach raibh iontach sásta go raibh Gaeilge acu. Ní maith le páistí a bheith difriúil. An dearcadh a bhí ann ná dá dtiocfadh linn áit a fháil agus páistí a thógáil le Gaeilge, go mbeadh sin ina chuidiú ag na páistí. Ba ghnách le Brighid agus cúpla duine eile naíscoil a reáchtáil ar an Satharn i gCumann Chluain Árd. Clann ar bith a raibh páistí acu, tháinig siad uilig chuig an Chluain Árd maidin Shathairn. Cuireadh coiste ar bun nuair a bhí siad ag dul a thógáil scoile. Tharla na Trioblóidí ag an phointe sin. D'éirigh linn sórt chalet a fháil. Nuair a bhí na Trioblóidí ann, cuireadh daoine isteach i chalets ar Bhóthar an Ghleanna agus nuair a d'éirigh leo dul ar ais chuig a dtithe féin nó tithe úra, bhí na rudaí seo fágtha agus d'éirigh linn ceann acu a fháil. Chuir muid ar an suíomh iad don chéad rang.

Bhí daoine againn ar an suíomh a raibh scileanna áirithe acu cosúil le Seán Mackel agus daoine eile. Ba é ailtire, Tom Ó Muineacháin, bhí Seán ina shiúinéir agus bhí Liam Ua Bruadair ina shiúinéir, agus bhí siadsan ábalta rudaí áirithe a dhéanamh.

Ní raibh taithí agam teagasc trí mheán na Gaeilge. Bhí cruinniú idir na múinteoirí Gaeilge i mBaile Átha Cliath agus ba ghnách liom dul ar cuairt acu siúd agus fáil amach faoi na leabharthaí a bhí siad ag úsáid agus an sórt sin. Chuaigh muid ar cuairt ar roinnt scoileanna.

Sa deireadh, chríochnaigh mise istigh ann le trí lá sa tseachtain agus Brighid Nic Sheáin dhá lá sa tseachtain. D'oibrigh muid mar sin é.

Nuair a dúirt tú go raibh scoil - 'Irish school' - agat, shíl daoine nach ndearna na páistí ach Gaeilge. Níor thuig siad go raibh siad ag déanamh Mata, Eolaíocht, achan sórt rud trí mheán na Gaeilge. Uair amháin nuair a thuig daoine sin, bhí níos mó suime acu na páistí a chur ann. Caithfidh mé a admháil, ach amháin na tuismitheoirí a bhí sásta na páistí a thabhairt dúinn, ní bheadh scoil ar bith againn. Déantar dearmaid díofa, na daoine a raibh muinín go leor acu ionainn lena bpáistí a chur agus go bhfaigheadh siad scolaíocht mhaith, tá moladh mór tuilte acu siúd. Ní raibh Gaeilge acu féin.

Bhí roinnt daoine a raibh suim acu sa pholaitíocht a chuir páistí ann. Bhí daoine ann a raibh suim acu i sóisialachas agus a bheith neamhspleách ón rialtas a chuir páistí ann. Bhí daoine ann a raibh dúil mhór acu sa teanga ach nár éirigh leo í a fhoghlaim ach a bhí ag iarraidh í a fhoghlaim agus chuir siadsan na páistí ann.

Agus chuidigh na Trioblóidí sa dóigh seo. Bhí daoine ag iarraidh cultúr s'acu féin a bheith acu.

...that it would be of help to the children
Máire Mhic Sheáin

It was nothing new to raise a family with Irish but the people who did that, they were dispersed throughout the city. The children didn't meet up that often and they felt they were on their own. And some were maybe not very happy that they could speak Irish. Children don't like to be different. Our attitude was that if we could get a place and raise children with Irish, that it would of help to the children. Bríghid [Mhic Sheáin] and a few others used to run a nursery on Saturdays in Cumann Chluain Ard. Any family that had children, they all came to the Cluain Ard on a Saturday morning.

A committee was set up when they went to build the school. The Troubles began at that point. We were able to get a chalet of sorts. When the Troubles began, people were put into chalets on the Glen Road and when they were able to go back to their own houses or to new houses, these things were left and we were able to get one. We put it on the site for the first class. We had people on the site with certain skills like Seán Mackel and others. Tom Ó Muineacháin was an architect, Seán [Mac Seáin, Máire's husband] was a joiner and Liam Ua Bruadair was a joiner, and they were able to make specific things.

I had no experience teaching through the medium of Irish. Irish language teachers would meet in Dublin and I used to visit them and find out what books they were using and that sort of thing. We visited a number of schools. Eventually, I ended up in there three days a week and Bríghid Mhic Sheáin did two days a week. It worked like that.

When you said you had a school – an 'Irish school' – people thought that the children only learned Irish. They didn't understand that they were doing Maths, Science, everything through the medium of Irish. Whenever people realised that, they were more interested in sending their own children. I have to admit, but for the parents who were willing to send their kids to us, we would have no school. They are forgotten, the people who had enough confidence in us to send their children and that they would get a good education, they deserve great praise. They didn't speak Irish themselves.

There were a number of people who were into politics who sent their children. There were people who were interested in socialism and in being independent of the government who sent their kids. There were people who were really into the language but hadn't succeeded in learning it but yet wanted to learn it and they sent their kids. And the Troubles helped in this way. People wanted to have their own culture.

17 **People came out from every house**
Jim Watson

So many people moved out of Belfast, during the Troubles, into places like Bangor. I first moved to Bangor in 1968 but my heart was always very much up the Shankill. I was born and bred on the Shankill, and to me this is where home was and it's where home will always be. I have a very special affection for Belfast people. There's one incident that happened that I'll always remember. This is going back a bit. In 1963, in the winter of the heavy snow, it was really bad here. My sister died, tragically, in England at 24 years of age. Her husband was a chief petty officer in the Royal Navy, and I remember my mother and father had to travel over to Plymouth, and they were coming back with the body on the Friday and the funeral was that Saturday. There was 3 feet of snow in our street, and we lived in number 66 so we were quite a bit down the street. And I remember starting at that door with a small tailed shovel, clearing the snow away so that the hearse could get down. And people came out from every house with a shovel and cleared that street for 500 maybe 600 metres, to the Crumlin Road. To get the hearse down the street. I'll never forget that.

There is not the same sense of community in Bangor but I'm very fortunate in that I have a church community. When I was working in a factory in Newtownards a girl stopped me and she says to me, 'Jim, we're thinking of opening a Free Presbyterian Church in Newtownards. Would you be interested in going?' I says, 'I would'. She says, 'Look, there's a meeting in the Scout Hall'. That was about 42 years ago, and I remember going to that meeting that night and there was only a handful of us, and we started a church in Newtownards. And the friendships that I have built up over 40 years with a lot of the folk there is remarkable. I have a daughter who died nine years ago and the support we got was beyond….. I couldn't even explain it.

18 **Before the Shankill redevelopment started**
Sandra Gibney

Agnes Street was like a main street then. There were bars and shops. At the bottom of our street there was an electrical shop, and on the other side was a wee corner shop but it sold meat like a grocery shop. Facing that again there was a wee newsagent shop and a fruit shop. This was all at the bottom of Blaney Street. At the top where we lived, we lived nearer the Crimea Street end, there were garages at the side of our house. There was a wee scout hall facing the top of our street there. Sandcross Street would have been there then. So there was loads of stuff there. This is all before the redevelopment started when they knocked all the houses down.

19 **Féinmheas a thabhairt ar ais, an áit a atógáil iad féin...**
Seán Magaoill

Áit iontach imeallach a bhí i mBaile Uí Mhurchú. Bhí fadhbanna sóisialta go domhan ann agus neamart iomlán déanta ag an bhardas agus ag an rialtas ar an phobal sin. Eastát suimiúil a bhí ann ar bhealach ach bhí sé go hiomlán imeallach ó mhuintir Bhéal Feirste go fírinneach. An chéad chomhoibriú a rinne mé, bhí siadsan ag iarraidh cuidiú ó dhaoine. Bhí cuid mhór daoine ag teacht ó Queen's agus sin ag tabhairt comhairle daofa. D'aithin siadsan na fadhbanna a bhí ann, na fadhbanna sóisialta agus d'aithin siad na riachtanais go soiléir ach ní raibh rud ar bith a thiocfadh leo a chruthú. Shocraigh siad go ndéanfadh siad é sórt proifisiúnta agus d'iarr siad cuidiú ó Queen's University. Mhol siadsan go ndéanfadh siad suirbhé proifisiúnta ar an eastát faoi chúram Tony Spencer a bhí i mbun na Roinne Sóisialta. Le linn sin ag dul ar aghaidh, bhí airgead a dhíth leis sin a dhéanamh. D'aimsigh siad an chéad chéim a thiocfadh leo tabhairt le maolú a thabhairt ar chúrsaí an cheantair, le hionad pobail a thógáil. D'aimsigh siad seanbhothán adhmaid a bhí an RAF ag díol amuigh in Aldergrove. Bhí siad dul á cheannach seo. Rud a thiocfadh leo tógáil go measartha gasta. D'iarr siad ormsa dul amach agus an rud a scrúdú. Chuaigh mé amach agus foirgneamh measartha réasúnta a bhí ann, ach níor shíl mé gurbh é an chéim cheart le déanamh. Rud adhmaid, réamhdhéanta a dhéanamh nuair a bhí an méid oibre le bheith déanta sa cheantar. Mhol mé gan a cheannacht agus go ndéanfainn féin dearadh ar fhoirgneamh buan ceart. Bhí suíomh ar fáil ar an bhóthar.

Rinne mise dearadh d'fhoirgneamh a bheadh fóirsteanach do dhream óg nó do dhaoine fásta le traenáil a dhéanamh, áit le súgradh, áit le cumarsáid agus áit a thiocfadh a úsáid do gach gné den tsochaí. Bhí mé féin agus Séamus Mac Seáin ag plé cúrsaí Bhaile Uí Mhurchú. Bhí muid goitse leis an rud. An t-aon dóigh a dtiocfadh linn cuidiú leis na daoine seo ná cuid dá bhféinmheas a thabhairt ar ais, an áit a atógáil iad féin.

Giving back self-respect, rebuilding the place themselves...
Seán Magaoill

Ballymurphy was a very marginalised place. The social problems went deep and the corporation and government had completely ignored that community. It was an interesting estate in a way but it was completely cut off from the people of Belfast to be honest. The first collaboration I did, they wanted help from people. There were a lot of people coming from Queen's and giving advice. They identified the problems that existed, the social problems and they identified the needs clearly but there was nothing they could create. They decided to do it professionally and they asked for help from Queen's University. They recommended that they do a professional survey under the supervision of Tony Spencer who was in charge of the Sociology Department. While that was going on, money was needed for it to be done. They identified the first step they could take to alleviate things in the area, which was to build a community centre. They identified an old wooden hut that the RAF was selling out in Aldergrove. They were going to buy this, something that they could build fairly quickly. They asked me to go out and examine it. I went out and it was a reasonable enough structure, but I didn't think it was the right step to take. To build something wooden, prefabricated, when there was so much work to be done in the area. I proposed not buying it and that I would design a proper, permanent building. There was a site available on the road. I designed a building that would be suitable for young people or for adults to do training, a place to play, a place to chat and place that could be used for every aspect of society. Séamus Mac Seáin and I were involved in the Ballymurphy issue. We were absorbed in it. The only way we could help these people was to give back some of their self-respect, for them to rebuild the place themselves.

20 **We're a melody band**
Norman Hunt

Well, my father was a musician. He played a flute and he was in a band called the Hillview Rising Star which was formed in Hillview Street in the Crumlin Road. We just celebrated our 60th anniversary there. And from I was an early age all I knew was my father writing music out and teaching bands, and I was brought up with music. You couldn't buy manuscript paper in those days and my Da would get old bits of cardboard, maybe an old Daz box or a cornflakes box, and I drew the lines for him. And he was drawing the staves and writing the music. He wrote wee tunes. We're still playing them at the minute. He composed some of them, and some he knew, old war songs you would know, 'Pack up your Troubles' and 'It's a Long Way to Tipperary' and all that there. He wrote them all down just out of his head. He just played a wee bit, and then he would write the music down. And that's what life was like in the house. I was coming in about 4 o'clock from school and he would say to me, 'have two or three of them lines wrote out for me' because there was no photocopiers in those days, and you had to sit and write every single one of them.

I was an eight-year-old when I joined the band. And we were a melody band. We played Crown A-Z wooden flutes which you can't get now because they were made of African blackwood which you can't get now. The band was in what's called the NIBA which is the North of Ireland Bands' Association, and they hold a competition every year for melody bands which we were. And we also joined the flute band league. The flute band league had contests for kids, you had what's called an under

10 solo, an under 13 solo and an under 16 solo. You learnt the music, you just stood up and you played on your own. But most of the wee lads were out of the big senior bands, and they were playing these big silver flutes, and we had these wee wooden flutes, but my Da always said to me, 'you get a better tone out of the Crown A-Z than you do out of the big concert flute, as they call them'. And it proved right, because me and a mate went in for the under 13 solo and played a tune called the Skye Boat Song and, to our surprise, my mate won it. Tommy Horner you called him, and I was fourth. And my Da and all the band near went nuts. And that was about, I suppose, 1961.

So the band has been my life from that. The first time we won the all Ireland championship was 1964 or '65, in the Ulster Hall. We practised in Leopold Street, up the Shankill. Then we got a place in Albion Court, off Agnes Street, and we won most of our Championships there. We won nine championships in all. While we were doing that the Troubles had started, and a lot of the boys out of the band joined various organisations, and the ones in the band were thinking it was going to be a paramilitary band at the time, but my Da wouldn't have it. He said 'no, we're a melody band. We're staying a melody band. That's all it is', he says. So we still are a melody band. We still carry no flags or no regalia.

21 There was something starting then
Hugh Mornin

I can remember when the Queen Elizabeth Bridge was opened around in '66, and the Queen was over for the opening of the bridge. Terence O'Neill was Prime Minister in Northern Ireland and he had gone down to Dublin for talks with the Taoiseach down there. And my wife and I went down to see them. The cars came round the big roundabout there at the Short Strand, where the flyover comes over, and the Queen was in one car and then Terence O'Neill was in another car. And when his car came round they were booing him and jeering him. There was something starting then because he had gone off down to talk to people down in the south or have a conversation.

22 The GAA is part of my soul
Jude Whyte

I got involved in the hurling club in Queens University. It was a very….I mean the GAA is part of my soul and it comes from the late Frank Corr who was a south Antrim secretary. He was assassinated by the loyalists in the early '70s. And my uncle, Seamus Whyte, who took us to matches in the '60s. My first match was 1963, a hurling match. I've the honour of saying that I saw Antrim winning an all-Ireland in '69 as a ten year old fella in Croke Park when they won the under-21 football. And I saw them in 1971 in the intermediate hurling. I saw them in another all Ireland where they were actually beat, I think it was Roscommon or Mayo beat them. But the GAA isn't a sporting organisation to me. It's actually a way of life, and it's a political statement which I suspect many people south of the border would find hard to understand. I mean, up here, to carry a hurling stick around this town was a statement, nearly, and it was also a provocation. It still is a provocation to many people - that you're targeting yourself as a Republican, or a nationalist, or something like that.

23 Charlie, I'll give you my all for 90 minutes
Jackie Henry

When we moved to Highfield to live I went to school in Ballygomartin, and I couldn't get playing on the football team there so I had to play rugby until I left school. And from there I went on play for Manor Street Boys Club which is no longer in our area now. We had a fantastic side there, and from there I went on to play for Linfield. And then Charlie Tully, the great Irish, Celtic and Northern Ireland footballer, was manager of Bangor, and he came up into the Glencairn to see me. I remember it as well. And he says, 'I've been told to sign you Jackie, and I'll give you £30, will you sign?' Now this was back in 1967, 68. And I was standing with my Whiterock band uniform on, my blue beret and my orange sash. And he says, 'Will you sign?' And I says 'yes'. So I signed for Charlie Tully and I went down to Bangor with my Linfield scarf on and played for Bangor. We beat Linfield 3-2, and I scored two of them and he hugged me, and he says, 'I didn't think you would have done it', and I says, 'Charlie, once you're a blues man you're always a blues man, but I'm playing for you for 90 minutes and I'll give my life, my all for 90 minutes for Bangor.'

24 The first time I ever knew there was a difference
Donna McIllroy

I can remember ones coming to the door and saying to my Mammy, 'We'll not touch your house if you put your flag out, if you put a flag outside your house', and my mammy told them where to go, she says, 'You'll not tell me what to do, so you'll not'. But, as I say, I had a neighbour on either side, two old couples, one was a wee woman called Mrs Ritchie, she was a Protestant and the other one was a woman called Mrs Shannon, her and her husband, and I remember Mrs Shannon's husband dying and my mammy being in her house quite a lot. And then there was the first time that I ever knew that there was a difference because I overheard my mammy saying that Mrs Shannon had decided to move down to Cushendall, with everything that was going on, and my mammy was saying, 'I'm losing a really good neighbour and it's ridiculous, just because she's Catholic. You know, she's better to me than these ones are that are coming down telling me, 'Oh, I'll look after you if you put a flag out', you know, sort of, what they're saying is that we'll identify that you're Protestant. But my mammy was, you know, 'I don't care what you are. Take yourself off'.

25 August 1969
Beatrice Elliott

I remember the 13th August 1969. My husband, he was a great motorbike enthusiast and they always went up to see the practice, the Ulster Grand Prix practice, him and his brother and they came home that night and he said, 'There's trouble on the Springfield Road'. I think they were attacking the police station then – that was the thirteenth of August and then the fourteenth I think it was the factories and all got it, the Falls Road factories and all round that way and then the trouble just erupted. Then Bombay Street, it was attacked.
We were told the Catholics were coming down to put us out so my husband got me and my two children then up to Finaghy where my mother and father lived, they lived up in

Taughmonagh which was a mixed area and I stayed up there for two days. And I came back home and when I came back home I went round to North Howard Street because the Catholics were getting put out of their houses, the houses were burning, and I just stood shocked, I was more mesmerised than anything when I saw the police sitting with their shirts open, their ties hanging off them and they were exhausted. And the wee ferret cars, we called them then, the wee ferret tanks, they were driving about and people were taking their furniture out of their houses and just houses on fire.

26   The night of the smoke changed everything
Bill Henry

Pre Troubles we could have went anywhere in Belfast. I remember going to the football matches in the Grosvenor road, cutting across the Falls Road with my blues scarf and all on. Nothing said to you, not a dickey bird. Nothing, no trouble whatsoever. And then the Troubles all blew up. My mother and father, my two sisters and me, we always went to a place called Butlins in Mosney down south. We went there for about eight or nine years and I always remember coming home that night and my father said in the car, 'Jesus Christ, what is that?' All we saw was smoke coming up the motorway, that's when the Troubles started. And from that night onwards everybody's life changed. The like of going to the Grosvenor, you couldn't do that. Because obviously you were getting stoned. And vice versa, the ones going to Solitude up to Cliftonville's ground, you couldn't do that, everybody's life changed that night. For the worse for me, because I think I

lost an awful sense of community gathering. My father used to bring anybody he worked with into the house, and that was Catholics too. And they were always welcome, and they still are. But then they didn't come over to our house, and my father didn't go to their house, because it wasn't the norm then, they were segregated right away. And I think that's when everybody said, 'Right, we'll stay in our own wee patch.' To me that night coming up the motorway from our holidays, that changed everything, that changed everybody's life here. That night of the smoke, that was the change in Northern Ireland completely for everybody.

27   Ag atógáil Shráid Bombay
Seán Mac Seáin

An plean a bhí againn do thithe s'againne(tithe ar Ghaeltacht Bhóthar Seoighe), b'ionann an plean sin agus plean de chuid na dtithe ag Bombay Street. Bhí muid i ndiaidh sin uilig a fhoghlaim agus cibé rud a bhí muid ag foghlaim, bhog muid sin go dtí Bombay Street. Sílim gur duine de na Unionists a bhí ann, you know the 'we're going to bulldoze' crowd, dúirt siadsan go dtógfadh siad na tithe arís ceart go leor ach go dtógfadh siad tithe a tógadh i ndiaidh an Dara Chogadh Domhanda nuair a scriosadh cúpla ceantar thíos, Alexander Park Avenue, Tiger's Bay agus Arizona Street. Thóg siad na tithe beaga seo a raibh dhá sheomra iontu. Now they're nice wee houses, dhá sheomra, seomra cónaí agus… nice, deas, ach na daoine a raibh cónaí orthu sna seantithe, teaghlaigh mhóra a bhí iontu.

Bhí atmaisféar iontach ann, agus an rud a tharla, dúirt an Bardas ag an am sin, 'now, these are being build illegally, and we'll bulldoze them down'. Lean muidne ar aghaidh, bhí daoine maithe againne, Gaeilgeoirí a tháinig le chéile ach ní dóigh liom go raibh muidne ag smaointiú ar an dóigh sin, gur Gaeilgeoirí a bhí ann, tharla gur sin mar a bhí sé; Albert Fry, Tom Ó Monacháin, Seán Mac Goill, Ciarán Ó Catháin, Séamus de Napier, mé féin, Séamus, 'uncle Tommy Cobbly and all' mar a dearfá. Tháinig an pobal le chéile le rud éigin fiúntach a dhéanamh, agus bhí sé go hiontach ar fad. Bhí daoine ag teacht as achan chearn den tír. Bhí dream ann as Coalisland, bhí ceithre dhuine dhéag sa mhionbhus. Dár le daoine gur gimmick a bhí anseo, calling us Communists! Communists, you know! Pure Christianity is Communism.

Bhí dochtúir amháin a bhí mór le rá ar an bhóthar anseo, fear iontach maith, a bhí ina Phoblachtóir go fírinneach, tháinig seisean chugam agus dúirt sé, 'Sure what can I do for you?', agus dúirt mise, 'Well, do you know this, if you can get us 6,000 rough brick' so chuaigh seisean agus dhíol sé as 6,000 rough brick do na ballaí taobh istigh. Bhí fear amháin a thug dhá chis mhóra de bheoir, stout nó rud éigin, dúinn. Tháinig Tim Pat Coogan agus daoine ó, I couldn't tell you... China... where they're from, agus labhair siad linn. Labhair mise ar an cheamara leo, now it wasn't Chinese now, I must admit.

Rebuilding Bombay Street
Seán Mac Seáin

The plan we had for our houses (houses on Shaws Road Gaeltacht), that plan was the same as the plan for the houses in Bombay Street. We had just learned all that and whatever we were learning, we brought it to Bombay Street. I think it was one of the Unionists, you know the 'We're going to bulldoze you' crowd, they said that they're build the houses again right enough but that they would build houses that had been built after the Second World War when a few areas were destroyed, Alexander Park Avenue, Tiger's Bay and Arizona Street. They built these little two-room houses. Now they're nice wee houses, two rooms, a living room and... nice, but the people who lived in the old houses, they were big families.

There was a great atmosphere, and what happened was that the Corporation at that time said, 'Now, these are being built illegally, and we'll bulldoze them down.' We carried on, we had good people, Irish speakers who had come together but I don't suppose we thought about it like that, that we were Irish speakers, it just happened that that's how it was – Albert Fry, Tom Ó Monacháin, Seán Mac Goill, Ciarán Ó Catháin, Séamus de Napier, myself, Seámus [Mac Seáin, Seán's brother], 'uncle Tommy Cobbly and all' as you'd say. The community came together to do something worthwhile, it was absolutely brilliant. People were coming from all parts of the country. There was a group from Coalisland, there were fourteen people in the minibus. Some people thought it was a gimmick, calling us communists! Communists, you know! Pure Christianity is communism.

There was a doctor who was well known on the road here, a very good man, who was a true republican, he came to me and said, 'Sure what can I do for you?' And I said, 'Well, do you know this, if you can get us 6,000 rough brick...' So he went paid for 6,000 rough bricks for the inside walls. There was one man who gave us two big crates of beer, stout or something. Tim Pat Coogan came and people from... I couldn't tell you... China, where they're from, and they spoke to us. I spoke on camera to them, now it wasn't Chinese now, I have to admit.

28 **My mommy lost her neighbours**
Irene Glassey

Highfield, then, was mixed. We had Catholics and Protestants in our street. We had a Catholic woman living next door to us, a Catholic woman living facing us, and a Catholic woman further up the street, and then that changed. People put the Catholic people out of our street. I would have been about, maybe, 12 or 13 then and I didn't understand, but when I got older I realised that it wasn't right. So my mommy lost her neighbours, and it wasn't the people in the street who put them out, it was other people. And my dad, and men that lived in the street, tried to stop it, but the Catholic people went. And like, one of the Catholic women, Mrs Mulholland, who lived facing us, her son was in the British Army which was, to my mind as a teenager, ridiculous. This guy is in the British Army and they're still putting his mother out of her house. My mommy said they were always good neighbours. Mrs Mulholland was never out of our house. He would have brought mommy lovely presents wherever he was in the army, wherever he was stationed, he would have brought mommy back lovely presents, and my sister would have knocked about with him when she was younger. But it was just one of those things, you know, that happened when the troubles started, you know.

29 **The troops walking down the street in the middle of the road**
Ann Henry

When the Troubles started I was only a kid. We lived down the bottom of Conway Street, and Conway Street was probably about three-quarters Protestant and then the bottom was Catholic. I remember all the trouble on the Shankill, and the rioting, and our neighbour up the street, Mrs. Daglish, said to my mummy, 'Look, I'm going to my wee country house at the week end. Do you want me to take Anne with me?' It was in Stonyford, that's where her wee house was. It was the summer in 1969 and away we went. And remember, then there were no phones so Mrs. Daglish couldn't phone my mummy to say, 'Well Isobel, how's things going?' because you just listened to the news. But I do remember it was the weekend that the wee child, Rooney, was shot. And I remember Mrs. Daglish and us going, 'oh my god a wee child's been shot, a wee child's been shot'. And then I remember coming back, I think it was Sunday night, and the troops walking down the street in the middle of the road. Now that was scary, that was really scary. And then in 1971 my brother was shot. He was shot by the paratroopers. There was rioting in the Shankill, left, right and centre and he was shot, by the paratroopers. Fortunately he didn't die, but he was left paralysed. So the Troubles had a big impact on us as a family.

30 **Cad é mar a thig liomsa rud éigin a dhéanamh?**
Liam Ó Maolchloiche

Throid m'athair le linn an Dara Cogadh Domhanda. Seo an chéad uair a tháinig saighdiúirí Shasana chuig ceantar s'againne. Ní raibh mise ach trí déag ag an am. Tá teach s'againne ar bharr cnoic agus san oíche sin, tháinig na mílte, mílte saighdiúirí Shasana suas an cnoc. Bhí tanks acu, machine guns, spotlights, war dogs, agus gach rud mar sin. Mise trí déag, agus in aice le m'athair. Bhí a fhios aige cad é a bhí ann nuair a dúirt sé 'fascism'.

Creid é nó ná creid é, dúirt mé liom féin, caithfidh muid troid in éadan seo. Mí Aibreán 1970, chinn mé dul le fáil amach cad é mar a thig liomsa rud éigin a dhéanamh. Cén saghas rud? Níl a fhios agam. Ach ag an am sin, bhí a fhios agam gur mhaith liom rud éigin a dhéanamh.

How can I do something?
Liam Ó Maolchloiche

My father fought during the Second World War. This was the first time that British soldiers had come to our area. I was only thirteen at the time. Our house is at the top of a hill and that night, thousands upon thousands of British soldiers came up the hill. They had tanks, machine guns, spotlights, war dogs, everything like that. I was thirteen, and beside my father. He knew what was going on when he said, 'Fascism.'

Believe it or not, I said to myself, we have to fight against this. April 1970, I decided to go and find out how I could do something. What kind of thing? I don't know. But at that time, I knew that I wanted to do something.

31 **An bharacáid is greannmhaire**
Larry McGurk

Bhí bacanna ar na bóithre achan uile lá agus ní raibh tú ábalta siúl suas Bóthar na bhFál, sin an saol a bhí ann. An ceann a ba ghreannmhaire, bhí sin i Sráid Sorella, ag bun Pháirc Dunville. An rud a rinne siad, ghoid siad bus, thiomáin siad an bus isteach ansin thiontaigh siad an bus go dtí go raibh bun na sráide druidte. So nuair a bhí na daoine ag dul amach ag siopadóireacht, shiúil siad isteach ar dhoras amháin, suas taobh istigh den bhus agus amach an doras éigeandála.

The funniest barricade
Larry McGurk

There were barricades on the road every single day and you couldn't walk up the Falls Road, that's what life was like. The funniest one, that was in Sorella Street, at the bottom of Dunville Park. What they did was, they stole a bus, they drove the bus in and then they turned the bus so that the bottom of the street was closed. So when people were going out shopping, they walked in one door, up in the bus and out the emergency door.

32 **Becoming involved in republican struggle**
Seamus Finucane

The experiences of 69 cut a deep wound in my parents. There was no party politics or history of politics in our family per se and we lived on the Protestant side of the peace line. We lived in Percy Street at this stage in '68 and '69. We witnessed the events leading up to the pogroms that unfolded. I can remember that in the lead up to it there had been sporadic events of mobs coming down from the Shankill. They attacked the priest's house, they attacked shops in Divis Street, and they tried to get into an old republican's house which also had lodgers. This was '68 into '69. Then on the 14th August 1969 we heard the screaming. We were terrified. We armed ourselves with hammers and hatchets. We were waiting on them coming in to attack us, and fortunately that didn't happen, although it did happen to our neighbours. When we were at the front door the next morning we were blatantly told to get out or we would be burnt out later that day. The fighting was so intense in Divis Street that we ended up getting a British

Army escort up through the Shankill and up into the upper Springfield where we stayed, with family friends, in the Dermott Hill area. Later we were rehoused in the Andersonstown area. We were squatting and then we moved to Lenadoon. The next big occasion in my life was the Falls' curfew. People from the Falls Road were evacuated up into the local school, Oliver Plunkett. I think events like this were starting to crystallise things in my life, and then I fell into the company of an older republican. He started talking to us about republicanism. It happened during a hostelling trip. A next door neighbour friend of mine and I went up to North Antrim and we bumped into a character from the Falls area. We just started talking about recent events within our community and how they impacted on us. I suppose I didn't comprehend or appreciate the degree of this person's involvement in the republican movement, but this was my first formal contact with anyone like that. Obviously at a young age we were very impressionable so we agreed to meet him again. Fortunately, or unfortunately, the meeting never took place. But I think my curiosity had been awakened by that stage and we decided to make our own inquiries locally. This is when the process began. I hid it from my father for quite a while because he just would have went berserk. He would have been so protective of me as his son, and the family. Right up until the time of his death he never displayed any interest in politics, nor gave any encouragement to any of us to become involved in the republican struggle. On the other hand, when I told my mother what I had done she was overjoyed. She was very proud and glad that I had taken this step even as a tender 14 year old. While my friend from the street whose family had republican connections, his father was an old republican, they went absolutely berserk.

33 **You felt sorry for them**
Norman McMaster

There was a brave few Catholics worked down in the ship-yard. The time the Troubles started the stagers came round and put them all out. You felt sorry for them. They were going to their work, innocent people and you were trying to wire them off, 'away on down that way there, the stagers are coming in that way'. You felt sorry for them.

34 **A microcosm**
Sean Simpson

Our street was called Glenshane Gardens and there was only 28 dwellings in that street. Out of that 28 dwellings, right up to '69, possibly '70, there were two RUC men lived in the street, there were two British soldiers and there was two screws lived in that street. Later 8 men went to jail for their republican activities out of that street, and two people were killed. My brother was killed by the British Army, and one of my neighbours was assassinated by the loyalists with a possible SAS connection. So it's probably a microcosm of this area, maybe of West Belfast.

35 **Forbairt íde-eolaíochta**
Peadar Ó Cuinneagáin

Ní raibh téarmaí mar 'fenian' agus 'IRA' agus 'Fianna Éireann' ann, ní raibh siad ar an radar mar a deirtear. An rud is mó, Náisiúnaigh nó Poblachtánaigh, a bhí le cloisteáil i dtigh s'againne ná na seancheirníní; 'A Fine Girl ya are' agus 'MacNamara's Band'.

Nuair a bhí mé ar an phluid, ar agóid na pluide, sin nuair a chuaigh mé leis an pholaitíocht. Thosaigh mé ag tuiscint cad is polaitíocht na heite clé agus polaitíocht na heite deise, nualiobrálachas, Marxachas, a leithéidí sin. Bhí léachtaí agus cainteanna ann. Níl a fhios agam agus mé ag amharc siar cé chomh maith, nó cén caighdeán a bhí ann ach ba chuma liomsa mar bhí sin ina chuidiú iontach agam. Ó thaobh na Gaeilge de, bhí Leo Greene mar mhúinteoir agam mar bhí seisean béal dorais. Ba ghnách leisean an Ghaeilge a chur ormsa ar na píopaí agus amach an fhuinneog. Tháinig leithéidí Pat McKeown agus Bik agus Larry Marley agus bhí leithéidí Leo Greene agus Mackers ann, Tony McIntyre. Ba ghnách liomsa mo chuid Marxachais a fháil ó Mackers. Thosaigh muid ag foghlaim faoin Phoblachtánas, agus an cúig 'isms' a bheirtear le chéile le Poblachtánachas a thabhairt duit. Secularism, anti-sectarianism is araile.

Ideological development
Peadar Ó Cuinneagáin

There were no terms like 'fenian' or 'IRA' or 'Fianna Éireann', they weren't on the radar as you'd say. The main thing, nationalist or republican, that you'd hear in our house would be the old records, 'A Fine Girl Ye Are' and 'MacNamara's Band'.

When I was on the blanket, on the blanket protest, that was when I became political. I started to understand what left-wing politics and right-wing politics were, neoliberalism, Marxism, that kind of thing. There were lectures and talks. I don't know as I look back how good it was or what standard it was at but I didn't care because it was of great help to me. As regards the Irish language, Leo Green was my teacher as he was next door. He used to teach me Irish on the pipes and out the window. The likes of Pat McGeown and Bik [Brendan McFarlane] and Larry Marley arrived and there was the likes of Leo Green and Mackers, Tony McIntyre. I used to get my Marxism from Mackers. We started to learn about republicanism, and the five 'isms' that are put together to give you republicanism. Secularism, anti-sectarianism and so on.

36 I'll never forget the day that internment came
Anne Barkley

I'll never forget the day that internment came. The Brits came busting in here but they didn't lift Paddy. But a man from Dermott Hill, he couldn't get up to Dermott Hill, and he had to come here. He saw them and he was afraid, and he climbed over the fences to my house and I took him in. And another man called Mr. Quinn, Pius Quinn, he had to stay here all evening, till he got up finally that night. The next day I looked out through the wee window at the top of the stairs and the Brits had these two young lads, I didn't know at the time who they were, but they lived behind me here, and they were called Doyles. The Brits had chained them to that place where the resource centre is. Mrs. Doyle's two sons. The two of them were butchers. And they tied them there, and I said, 'Oh my god, they've got two boys, young lads, and I don't know what they're going to do with them.' I heard later that they got released anyway. But I'll never forget internment.

37 Internment
Gerry Fitzpatrick

I was interned twice. The first time I was brought to Crumlin Road gaol and was there for about two and a half weeks, then they brought us into the chopper and brought us over to Long Kesh. This was going on a daily basis. They had a launching pad and everything else. I was in Cage 2, Long Kesh. It was run like an army you know. You were told to do something, you done it. The prisoners organised it. The screws opened up the cell doors in the mornings and let you out, and you were closed in again at 10 o clock at night. You only saw them those two shifts, 8 o clock in the morning, 10 o clock at night. One was to let you out, the other was to lock you up. I got out in November 1971, and back in again in June 1972.

38 Two days after the introduction of internment
Sean Simpson

My brother was shot dead on the 11th of August, two days after the introduction of internment. He was an IRA volunteer although he wasn't on active service that day. He was actually married and lived down in the Clonard area but he had come up to see my mother. But the type of scally-wag he was, our Seamus, if he heard there was trouble he would have gone straight to it. And he knew there was trouble up around the Rosnareen area. There were barricades up and the British Army was there trying to get in. The IRA were still on the defensive at that stage. What my brother had in his hands that day was probably only a stone, and he carried the tricolour, and this is when the British Army shot him dead. I would probably say I was heading in the direction of republicanism at that stage anyway. After my brother was killed, in '71, I didn't know where to go. Then you start looking round and you see which mates are up to something. Why are they not playing football at the corner like they used to be? So I just put it straight to a couple of mates of mine. By the following year, by about the summer of '72, I joined the Fianna in Riverdale. My Fianna days were probably like a lot of people, continuous scouting, standing at street corners, blowing whistles, warning the people that the Brits were in the area. Rioting, continuously rioting, especially after Operation Motorman in 1972.

39 There were parts of Belfast that weren't being touched
Jo-Ann Harrison

The troubles changed lives for children that were my age. One minute you were out playing, happy, playing street games with other children and then all this started happening. The bombs were going off all over the place in Belfast, there was shooting, people were getting killed. It changed my life. When the army came in there started to be No Go Areas. The streets were all cordoned off, so we couldn't get out. I remember going round to Sunday School in Bellevue Street which was the next street from Canmore Street, and I remember looking up the Kashmir Road and seeing the children my age that we had played with. Then they started to throw stones at each other, so from then it was just like we hated one another because of what was going on. And I was frightened for my mum and dad. My daddy worked in the linen mill up in Flax Street, just off the Crumlin Road, and I didn't want my daddy to go out anywhere, the same with my mum. In my early teens I joined a running club with a couple of friends. We would have got the Lisburn Road bus up to the Mary Peters Track. We got the bus at the City Hall and we met other fellas and girls the same age as ourselves, but they came from areas that weren't having any trouble. They couldn't believe what we were seeing and hearing at night in bed. They didn't really know what was going on. There were parts of Belfast that weren't being touched.

40   Mackie's was going 24 hours a day
Drew Johnston

I left school at 15. I applied for an apprenticeship to Mackie's in 1965. In November I got word that I was accepted. I did the medical in December, and I left school the week coming up to Christmas. I started off my employment in James Mackie and Sons, the biggest textile and engineering company in the world, with over 8000 workers in it, not all at the one time, different shifts. But it was going 24 hours a day, different parts of the factory. And I was there until I had to come out with ill health in 1990, and I enjoyed it. I was a fitter, a textile fitter. I worked in the hard fibre department which was the first process of machines that cut the jute, threaded the jute, split it before it went on to the carding frames. So they were producing bags in those days, jute bags and backing for carpet. Most of it went to Pakistan because it was a large jute growing country, and rice and food stuffs and grain were put into jute bags and shipped across the world. And then the Troubles. You couldn't go here and you couldn't go there because of road blocks. You were maybe an hour trying to get from one side of the town to the other because of the road blocks, which were essential to stop the bombers coming in. So you lived with it. You had to live with it. A friend of mine out of Mackie's lost both legs in the Abercorn bomb, Jimmy Stewart from the Woodvale area. So it was starting to affect people that you knew. Many a time in Mackie's you had to get out. We had to be protected to get home along Cupar Street at night by the army and the police because we were coming under attack by stones. And on two occasions they fired on the workers coming out of Mackie's and injured three of them. So it was starting to affect you in your work then too. Not only in your social life but when you were going to work and coming out of work. Then in the 90s the industry started to close down. ICI closed, Michelin closed their factory in Craigavon, the shipyard lost a lot of men. So there was a lot of people getting put on the dole queues. Mackie's first pay-offs came in the early '90's.

41   There will be a day of reckoning
Mary Kelly

It was bad enough they shot him, but they took his character. They said he was an IRA gunman organising the crowd. That nearly killed my mummy and daddy because of the way we were brought up. It nearly killed us all because it put us in an awful situation. It left my brothers wide open for paramilitary groups to say, 'well one was IRA, they all are'. So that was what we had to live with, and us knowing that he was an innocent critter out working every day. Michael had just turned 22. He had a wee motor scooter and he was saving up for a motorbike. And him and my da were always out the back, fixing at the car and the wee motor scooter. He never went to the clubs or anything.

I'll never forget coming home from the hospital the night Michael died, because my wee brother Paul was with me and the doctor gave him an injection. We were coming home and I could feel this dampness. I was carrying Michael's clothes, and when I got into the house the blood was in Michael's boots and it was all running down me. To this day I can still smell the blood. That has stayed with me, and when I saw the heartache of everybody crying I thought, 'Oh my God. Never forget it. Let us never forget it because you don't want that all happening again. You just don't.'

My attitude then was that we could do nothing, but my father went everywhere and went to see people, but then he said, 'That's the way it is'. And about a year before he died he said to me, 'You know, these Troubles can't go on forever. There will be a day of reckoning here somewhere.' And he said, 'Mary, you're the one to do it.'

So when I was approached to do a TV programme for the BBC it gave me a way to highlight Michael, to highlight what happened to him, and that he was innocent. And then I had to do about three or four years with the HET, the Historical Enquiry Team that was set up by the Government. Nobody realises the time I had with them and the work to do to get his name cleared. One thing that didn't sit right with me is that they said it was a patrol that was coming up the street, and I said, 'Well, why you are not interviewing that patrol?' They said 'He doesn't want to talk to you.' I didn't think that was right. But then at the time I thought, 'Well you know what, it won't bring him back. As long as I get his name cleared.'

My mummy and daddy were thinking of moving just prior to that happening, but they stayed there. What was the use in moving now that Michael had died? My father was able to buy a grave and put a headstone on it. And till they died they went every week to the graveyard. Every week those two went faithfully to the graveyard. Now they are buried with Michael. All their names are on the headstone.

42 I miss you such a great deal but I'm still your mother
Joan Linhart

Peter was 19 and Junior was 20. And on the 4th July they got ready and went to visit their friends. They went out together because Rosaleen lived off the Cliftonville Road and Peter's friend, John, lived round the corner from there. Off they went and Frank and I were sitting watching TV and David, the youngest, was outside with some of his friends from around the area. It was later on a neighbour of ours came up, a Mr. Osborne, a very gentlemanly kind of a person, and he said to me, 'Mrs. Orr, I'm sorry to trouble you but there's a phone call for you down at our house.' Of course in those days not many people had a phone. So it was my son's girlfriend, Rosaleen, she says, 'Has Junior left home?' I said, 'Yes'. She says, 'Well, Mrs Orr, he's not here', and I could kind of hear panic rising in her voice, and I says to her, 'He'll turn up, my love, it'll be alright'. So I thanked Mr. Osborne and came home and told Frank. Rosaleen had said she'd gone around to the Kelly's, that was John's name, John Kelly, and Peter hadn't arrived there either. So Frank said, 'I'm going out to find them'. So we went down the road which we thought they would have taken and we got to Rosaleen's house. We didn't stay long because we wanted to go round to see John. His mother was at the door and she was really worried. She said,

'Pete's not come, Pete's not come'. They called him Pete. And then we went to the Oldpark Police Barracks to report them missing. And the policeman said, 'What's their age?' Frank said 19 and 20, and the policeman put his pen down, he said, 'I can't put that down in the book'. He said, 'Have you any idea how many boys go missing in the city at night?' and Frank's words were, 'I don't care how many boys go missing', he said, 'I'm telling you, my sons are missing. Because when they go out they tell us where they're going, and they never reached their destination.' Then we went home and my mother-in-law, my brother-in-law, my sister-in-law and my nephew came round. The two Raymonds both went out in the car looking for them. We stayed up all night and then dawn broke. Raymond knew I was awake and he said to me, 'Do you want to go out?' and I said 'yes'. He drove me and we went down to the Mater Hospital, and between us we described the boys and the nurse said, 'Oh I wish I could help you, that's the third time somebody has asked about those two boys'.

And we went home and I think it must have been on the half ten news, because in those days they gave out a news bulletin every hour on the half hour, and it came right at the very, very end of the news, 'and in Northern Ireland, the bodies of two men have been found off the main airport road', and I said to Frank, 'That wouldn't be anything to do with us', I said, ' because they would have said young men'. He said, 'Yes, I know', and I said, 'They would have even said maybe youths, and again he agreed with me, but he got up from his chair, and he said, 'I can't stick it any longer, I've got to go back to the police barracks'. So Raymond took us to the police barracks, and we went in and Frank said, 'Last night we reported our two sons missing and they've found the bodies of two men off the main airport road', and the policeman said to him, 'No, that's nothing to do with you, Mr. Orr', and I stood and I put my hands like that and I said, 'Thank God, thank God, thank God', and then I said, 'God help somebody, they're going to get some awfully bad news today'. And we were almost on our way out, we were right at the door, when we were called back and it was two plain detectives, and one of them bent forward and said, 'You know you've got to be very, very brave,' he said, 'it could be 99% your sons', and do you know, it never registered, it did not register. Not with me.

But if it hadn't been for my faith in God I wouldn't be here now. He has helped me all the way, when I didn't even know it. You know, sometimes after the death of my sons I didn't even want to speak to people, I didn't know who to trust, and I remember one night there was somebody murdered, and I said to my husband, 'That's what your – your people - did to my sons,' and very quietly he said to me, 'Joan, they were my sons too'. I was so eaten up with grief, and I suddenly thought to myself, if Junior and Peter walked in now they wouldn't know me, I'm not the mother they knew. And from then on I went out and decided to look for the best in people. And tonight I'll tell them about my day, because their photographs are there, and I'll tell them about my day and I'll tell them that I love them, and I just pray, say a little prayer, and then I pick up each photograph and I kiss it. And I'll look right into the photograph and I'll say, 'Junior, I love you, I love you so much, my love, and I miss you such a great deal, but I'm still your mother, I'm still Mum, and to me you're still my kind and gentle son'. And then with Peter I'll say the same thing, but with Peter I'll say, 'I'm still your mother, I'm still Mum, and to me you're still my kind and smart young son', because my Peter loved nice things, he liked good clothes, and around that time there was a tailor business at the beginning of Royal Avenue, and they made made-to-measure suits, and Peter was saving up for a made-to-measure suit.

My attitude is, unless you're a very, very strong character, you can't help who you fall in love with. I would have followed Frank Orr to the end of the world. I mean we were married for just over 26 years and I loved him all those years, you know, and when Junior told me about Rosaleen, that she was a Roman Catholic, how could I turn around and say, 'No, you mustn't do that'. I came from the Channel Islands to marry my husband, because I loved him, and I know my son was so in love with her, so very in love with her.

It was very, very hard for Frank. I remember, evening after evening after evening, I would get up to put on the light and he would make some excuse and one night, I don't know whether I had a bit of sewing to do or something, and I says, 'Frank, I've had enough of sitting in the dark all the time,' and I just got up and turned on the light, and the tears were running down his cheeks. He used to cry softly so that I didn't hear with the noise of the TV. I always said Frank Orr died of cancer - and a broken heart.

43 **He died a week later**
Betty Morrison

I was working in the British Home Stores and it was blown up. The Monday after Bloody Sunday, that was. And I says to my friend, 'we'll be in and out of here today in bomb scares because we've British up in the letters outside'. And I had no sooner said it, it was 5 past 9, the bells went. I worked up on the first floor in the electrical department - that was all your lights and wall lights. So the staff had to sweep forward to make sure the customers were out, and I went behind the staff to make sure the staff were out. And we got outside and down round the corner and one of the other floor managers come down, and he says, 'It is a bomb'. And here's us, 'it'll not be, it'll not be'. We were only out by the skin of our teeth. We were just out and round the corner and the thing went up. The bomb was actually in that wee alley that you can go down through into High Street. And our assistant manager was going from the clothes end over into the food hall, and the window cleaner's van was parked right in the middle of the alley. And when he got in the other side he says, 'They don't park that van there, what did he park that van there for?' And he went back and looked in the back window and he saw the bomb. And if he hadn't have we would have been in the shop when it went up. But one of the other staff was killed. Paul McFadden you called him. We were all put down to the bottom towards Littlewoods, but he had gone to the top of that wee arcade the other way. He was helping people away from the arcade and as he turned to go back the bomb went off. He died a week later, left two wee children. He was a Catholic so we all went to the chapel for his funeral. And the children were really young then, I'd say 3 or 4, about that age. And I often wonder, they could have families of their own and all now.

44 **The Abercorn bomb**
Donna McIlroy

I was seven. Every Saturday me and mammy used to go down town, it would have been a wee treat, we would have went into the Abercorn restaurant for lunch. Me and my mammy went in as normal and sat down. I remember they always used to have one of these cake trolleys and I could pick my bun. I said to my mammy, 'I need to go to the toilet', and I went to the toilet at the back of the restaurant. I can remember hanging my bag on the back of the door and just sitting on the toilet and the next minute everything was all smoky. I could feel something at my back, I pulled my trousers up, I didn't know what had happened. I didn't hear a bang, I was thinking 'what's going on?' The door had been blown off and was hanging slanty, you know, horizontal. And looking at my wee handbag and thinking my handbag had been ripped… 'My good handbag', but still not having any sense of what had even happened. I couldn't really see right, it was very dusty and foggy.

I could hear this man shouting, 'Is there a wee girl called Donna in there?' you know, and I stood for a wee minute and I thought, 'He must be talking, he must be asking for me, how would he know I was in here', and then I thought, 'Mammy must have sent him'. So I shouts, 'yes I'm in here'. And he shouted, 'Can you come over to me? Can you get through to me?' and I remember looking at the big glass wall and that all being totally shattered, you know, and not being able to really see anything. He kept shouting, 'Come to me, come to me, I'll get you out'. So I got to him and I was able to climb up and over and whatever, and he lifted me up in his arms and had me and he was saying, 'Your Mammy's here, your Mammy's alright'. So what had actually happened was, this man had been passing outside in the street whenever the bomb had went off and he had come in, he'd stepped into the building to try to help people, to try to get people out, and he had seen my Mammy just standing in the middle, just screaming, 'My child, my child'.

So whenever I got out then she did see me at one point and he said to her, 'Now you hold on to the back of me and follow me'. So we made our way out down to the front and then there was a soldier at the window, and he passed me through to the soldier who then took me over to Evans' outsize shop that used to be in the corner. But when he passed me to the soldier, I looked behind, I didn't know where my Mammy went. Apparently what had happened, she had blacked out and she had no recollection of him finding me. So she actually climbed back in to go and look for me.

So I was in Evans' and they were bringing people in and out, and I was lying and I was looking and I was thinking, 'How's my Daddy going to know where we are? How's my Daddy going to know what's happened?' and I thought, 'What am I going to do if they don't find my Mammy?' And there was this woman, she worked behind the counter. She came over and was sort of sitting with me, talking away and I remember thinking, 'I wonder will she take me home with her, I don't know whether I want to go home with her and live with her'. These were the sort of crazy things that were going through my mind, you know. And then I said to her, 'Look, my Mammy's going to be worried about me. I'm going to have to go and find her'. And she was saying, 'No. No. You have to stay here', but she went out into the street and found a female police or a female soldier or something and she was saying, 'Look, this wee girl wants to go and find her Mammy', and I just says, 'because she'll be really worried about me, so she will, because she'll not know where I am'. She took me. So we started going into the wee shops to look for her, and she was asking me, 'Was she able to walk?' and stuff, I suppose, trying to decipher, you know, is she alive or is she dead or what. So then we got up and there was this wee carpet shop. It was one of these long, long shops and I said, 'Yes, there she is and my Mammy was just sitting on a pile of all the samples at the back absolutely breaking her heart. And I went in and I says, 'Look, we're alright now'.

45 The black taxis were always in the middle of everything
Breige Brownlee

To me the black taxis are just synonymous with everything that is West Belfast. My first vision of a black taxi was years ago when I was very young, I was about 10 and it was my first venture out on my own into town. And the next thing there was something going on. I didn't know what it was, I had heard bangs earlier. It was my first personal experience of anything and there were cars flying past, there were ambulances flying past, and the next thing I saw a black taxi flying past the bus stop. And there were people in the back of the black taxi and the horn was going to make people move aside. I remember seeing somebody in the back of the taxi with blood pouring out of them. That was my first black taxi experience and that was the day that Kelly's bar at the top of the Whiterock was bombed. After that, black taxis, to me, were always in the middle of everything. Everything that happened in the community. When the Ulster Workers' Strike was on, there were black taxis on the road. When there were bombs, when the buses were off the road, the black taxis were on the road. When there were bomb scares and people had to get out of their houses, black taxis were there taking people to community centres. And that was my whole impression of the black taxis. And apart from their community involvement they're also the only source, or were the only source, of employment for a lot of people as well. For ex-prisoners, for republicans, for people with names like Kevin Barry who couldn't go anywhere else, black taxis were a brilliant source of employment. I don't think they have been recognised enough for that source of employment, and the contribution that they make to the economy.

46 That was our defiance
Hugh Mornin

Our kids were small and we were walking down the Newtownards Road with our Lorraine in the pram, going down to my mother's house in Solway Street. We walked down and you could just hear the explosions, and you saw the bits of smoke coming up around the city on Bloody Friday. You got in and you listened to the radio and you heard about the 13 bomb explosions or whatever going off. Then we heard about that wee fella Parker who got killed. He went round to tell people about the bomb being there and he got killed in the explosion. We never missed a Saturday going into town. We went into the city every Saturday with our kids and went round to the Co-Op, as it was then. In other words, you're not going to put us off. Our defiance was going about our normal life, going into town, shopping or whatever. That was our defiance. You weren't going to put us off.

47 His hands in his pockets
Roy Harris

I was standing no more than 5 or 10 feet from Andrew Petherbridge when he was shot dead. Andrew Petherbridge was shot out of a Saracen driving past, and he had his hands in his pocket, and he was hit right in the head. He was only a kid. They tried to say he was rioting. There wasn't even a stone thrown that day. That wee fella was lying with his hands still in his pocket and the policeman came over, I turned round and said to him, 'I hope you realise this wee fella's hands are in his pockets'. That's the way he fell, with his hands still in his pockets.

48 My dad never recovered from it
Ally Kennedy

My dad had mental health problems but he got himself sorted out, he became a taxi driver and he loved his job. And then he was hi-jacked and had to drive a bomb into Bangor police station. He got out and shouted, 'Bomb!' Thank god the thing didn't go off. But they kept my dad for a good few days, I think because he might have been in danger. To me, that took my childhood away because my dad had a breakdown and never recovered from it. He wouldn't go out of the house, he was scared. If any of my friends came to the house he was actually like a baby, he went and hid in the corner. He ended up a schizophrenic, was afraid to come out of the house. So I lost all my childhood days with my father because of the Troubles.

49 I'm at home on this road
Bobby Connolly

I'm 40 years on the road now. Many a time I said to the wife, I wish I was ten years younger. I don't want to stop because I'm me and the taxi, and that's me, and I'm at home on this road. I get up at half five every morning, and I'll be in Poleglass at quarter past six, first pick up. There's regulars there. The people out there are great people, unbelievable. I think they're brilliant. What they were going through in the '70's, getting into our taxis and standing waiting for us. They got into our taxi and they knew one way or another we'd get them home. Sometimes you'd have to drive away up to Hannahstown and away down the Hannahstown hill into Lenadoon. And people never said, 'Where are you going driver?' They never queried us. They had great faith in us. I never was afraid on this road. I was just at home here as I am today. As happy as the day grows long. I just fell in love with it, it was my job and I loved it, as I still do today.

50 An chéad mhúinteoir a bhí agam
Pilib Ó Ruanaí

An chéad mhúinteoir a bhí agam ná Eddie Fay. Is de Lóistín an Móna i mBéal Feirste Eddie agus tá sé ag tiomáint tacsaí dubh sa lá atá inniu ann. Sin an chéad mhúinteoir a bhí agam le linn agóid na pluide. Riamh anall, bhí sórt fonn orm nó bhí mé ag santú na Gaeilge. Ní dhearna muid Gaeilge ag an mheánscoil, rinne muid beagán Gaeilge ar an bhunscoil agus is cuimhin liom gur bhain mé bonn i bhfeis Bhéal Feirste as dán a aithris agus bhí an bonn sin ar uaireadóir m'athair go dtí an lá sin a fuair sé bás. Bhí dáimh agam leis an Ghaeilge agus bhí fonn orm an rud a fhoghlaim. Ní raibh an deis ann go dtí an t-am sin agus nuair a tháinig an deis, rinne mé amach go ndéanfadh mé mo sheacht ndícheall, máistreacht a chur ar an Ghaeilge. Sin an rud a rinne mé, bhí mé iontach dícheallach ag an am sin.

My first teacher
Pilib Ó Ruanaí

My first teacher was Eddie Fay. Eddie is from Turf Lodge in Belfast and drives a black taxi today. He was my first teacher during the blanket protest. I had always had an interest because I had a thirst for the Irish language. We didn't do Irish in secondary school, we did a wee bit of Irish in primary school, and I remember that I won a medal in a Belfast Feis for reciting a poem and my father had that medal on his watch until the day he died. I loved the language and I wanted to learn it. I didn't have the chance until that time when the opportunity arrived, I decided to do my very best to master the Irish language. That's what I did and I was very diligent at that time.

51 **I'm not walking by you**
Ruby Hill

I really had a lot of Catholic friends when I was young. One girl Mary and I went away to the Isle of Man for three months together. And I have a story about Mary. When I was in Ballybeen and my Billy was only a wee born baby, and with a new born baby you have to put powder on their belly, and I tried every doctor in Ballybeen but his belly wasn't better, and the button or clip you put on just didn't work. So I decided to go back to my doctor off the Grosvenor Road. So when I got up there it wasn't there anymore. And somebody told me it's moved to Donegal Road. So I went around to Dr Sloan on the Donegal Road, and I went in and I said that I used to be a patient and I'd like to see Dr Sloan. So they told me to wait my turn and I looked over and I saw my chum Mary with her husband. They were waiting. She had a wee kid with her. We were very close friends and I felt a little choke in me, and she looked over and she turned away, and I turned away because I didn't want to get her into trouble with her husband. Mary was called first with her husband and child and they went up the stairs. After the buzzer went I was next to go up, and as I went up the stairs they were coming out of the doctor's office and she put her arms around me and said, 'I don't care what he says, I'm not walking by you!' And I said 'that's good Mary, because I love you too'. And she just hugged me. It broke her heart that day to see me and not be able to talk to me, but she couldn't go on. I knew I mustn't say anything because of her husband. If she'd been on her own I'd have gone over to her, but I knew not to do that.

52 **Bhí an troid sin i gcónaí ann**
Caoimhín Mac Mathúna

Is cuimhin liomsa bheith gníomhach sna Fianna agus lá amháin gur fhan muid amach as an teach thar oíche. Comóradh d'imtheorannú a bhí ann. An mhaidin sin bhí beirt againn ann agus droma mór peitril againn. Stop muid veain a tháinig thart ar an timpeallán thíos ag Musgrave, in aice le Musgrave Park Hospital agus m'athair a bhí ag tiomáint an veain! GPO veain a bhí ann agus dúirt mise leis, 'We're taking your van!' and he says, 'You're not!'. Lig mé dó agus thiomáin sé ar aghaidh agus níos moille sa lá sin nuair a chuaigh mé isteach sa teach thosaigh sé ag argóint liom agus ag tabhairt amach domh agus ag caitheamh maslaí ormsa. Ar ndóigh, shéan mé gur mise a bhí ann!

Bhí mé i gcónaí ag troid le m'athair fá dtaobh de chúrsaí polaitíochta agus ag argóint. Is cuimhin liomsa fiú nuair a bhí mé ag cur isteach ar phostanna agus má bhí ceist ann fá do chuid náisiúnachais, is cuimhin liomsa iad a rá liom go gcaithfidh tú cur síos gur Briotanach thú, agus bhí mise a rá, 'ní thig liom sin a dhéanamh'. Cé gur rugadh i Sasana mé, ach níor amhanc mé orm féin mar Shasanach. Shíl mé riamh gur Éireannach a bhí ionam de thairbhe mo chuid tuismitheoirí agus achan rud eile, nach raibh mé i Sasana le dhá bhliain.

Dhiúltaigh mise sin a scríobh. Scríobh mise i gcónaí gur Éireannach mé agus bhí a rá, 'ní bhfaighidh tú an post', ach bhí mise ar nós cuma liom. Bíodh sin mar atá, is cuma liom. Bhí an troid sin i gcónaí ann.

There was always that fight
Caoimhín Mac Mathúna

I remember being busy in the Fianna and one day we stayed away from home overnight. It was the anniversary of internment. That morning there were two of us and we had a big petrol drum. We stopped a van that came around the roundabout down at Musgrave, beside Musgrave Park Hospital and my father was driving the van! It was a GPO van and I said to him, 'We're taking your van!' and he says, 'You're not!' I let him go and he drove on and later that day when I went home he started arguing with me and giving out to me and insulting me. Of course, I denied that it was me!

I was always fighting with my father about politics, and arguing. I remember even when I was applying for jobs and if there was a question about your nationality, I remember them telling me that you had to put that you were British, and I said, 'I can't do that.' Even though I was born in England, I didn't see myself as English. I always thought that I was Irish because of my parents and everything else, that I was only in England for two years. I refused to write that down. I always wrote that I was Irish. They said, 'You won't get the job', but I didn't care. Be that as it may, I don't care. There was always that fight.

53 **The big strike**
Norman McMaster

I was 25 at the time of the big strike in '74. I loved that big strike, walking about there as if you owned the place. It was brilliant. Just walking down the Woodstock. I remember we lifted rubbish for the people. Big Norman Beattie was driving the big bin lorry and there was two of us on the back throwing the rubbish in. It kept all the aul dolls happy. And then we had a wee hut on the Woodstock there. Tommy McClure used to cook us stuff. He threw everything into the soup. The soup was brilliant. It was brilliant, that summer.

54 **You went in reading the Beano and came out reading Karl Marx**
Kevin Carson

They call Long Kesh the University of Freedom, and I learned more in Long Kesh, in those couple of years, than I ever learned in any school, or any form of work, or job, or anywhere else. I learned to be politically aware. I learned about all the different struggles around the world, and who was fighting the Brits here, and who was fighting the Americans there. You became politically aware, and you knew what every regime was in every country in the world, and you knew who the real bad guys were and who the real good guys were. You read things from Che Guevara, Karl Marx, Franz Fanon. We would have read British anti-insurgency manuals. A lot of the stuff was smuggled into the Kesh, or you got the covers changed and made them out to be stupid books, to look like just ordinary novels, but they were actually… And in them days every cage had to have a Gaeltacht hut, and everybody spoke Gaelic in it or learned Gaelic in it. If you didn't want to learn the Irish then you went to what we called the wasters' huts. The other two huts. So the political hub would be in the Gaeltacht hut because that's where all the thinkers were, so to speak. So you went in reading the Beano and came out reading Karl Marx, that's the way I saw it.

55 Like it was yesterday
Joan Johnston

I used to think to myself, we were the Harvey's and we were untouchable because nothing would happen to us, because we were such a happy family and got on and never done anybody any harm . That's what my thoughts were and then when Shughie was murdered that was a whole different ball game. We thought that would never happen to us. And Hugh was such a harmless soul. He was a pig farmer, he worked out in Carryduff and never done anybody any harm. He was out with his girl one night and was blew up in the town. And it was never the same. My mammy couldn't cope, she couldn't go back to work. It was just awful. She just…. And my dad was devastated, absolutely. But there was no help, none. It's forty years but it's so, so fresh, like it was yesterday.

56 Internment overrode everything
Roy Harris

I was interned in 1973. After I was lifted they let me go, out of Mountpottinger. The solicitor at that time was Harry Hall and he said to me, 'By the way, when you go out through the gates, you will be arrested and interned'. When I walked out the gate I was interned. They put us into Compound 11, and there was about seven UVF men and there was another five UDA men interned in front of me. You were there and you didn't know why you were there. I was in six weeks before I was handed allegations about why I was there. And the allegations that they were making were a complete joke. They brought you into a commission. The commissioners sat at the bottom, and at one corner there was a big curtain across, just like a hospital curtain, right across a door. You weren't allowed to speak. There was only your barrister and solicitor. The Commissioner was called Mr Leonard. He was a retired judge from the Old Bailey. And they called the first witness, and the next thing the door opened and there was a big pair of boots just sitting underneath the curtain, and the voice came out like a Dalek. I turned round to Desmond Boal and I said, 'What's that?' And he said, 'Wait till you see'. And he just turned round, just like a Dalek would talk, through a speaker, 'This man is a known terrorist in the Newtownards Road and that's all I would like to say about him', and the next thing the door closed. That was the witness. You were not even allowed to cross question him. Then they brought another one in, and he started talking and the same thing. And your man Leonard said to Mr Boal, 'I'm going to permit you to question this witness', and when Desmond Boal questioned him, he said, 'I'd like to give my evidence in camera'. Once he said that the solicitor, barrister and me were put out. You were brought back a half an hour later. Leonard turned round and said 'What was said about your client was very, very bad' and that was it. You weren't allowed to question, to ask him what about this and what about that. They asked me if I wanted to be charged legally through a Diplock Court or did I want to continue. And Desmond Boal said, 'No, we'll go outside to a Diplock Court'. And we went out and fought these charges in court, and I beat them and I was still brought back to internment, because interment over-rode everything. The other ones in the dock that weren't interned went straight home and we were brought back to the compound. About five weeks later I got another hearing with the same judge. When I went in front of him he turned round and says, 'There is no reason this man should be here because he went out and fought this in a legal court of law. There is nothing I can do about this. He has to be released'. They didn't want me let out, and Leonard turned round and said, 'I'm not accepting that'. He said, 'Take the handcuffs of this man, he is going home right now'. And that was me out.

57 Mrs Hill accuses Secretary of State William Whitelaw
Ruby Hill

When my husband was interned that was the first time I walked into the UDA headquarters, and there were parcels for me to take up, and the bus was on for me to go visit, kids and all.

And then the treasurer came round on a Friday night, and he would have given me an envelope with £12, I think. That was a lot of money to me then. And he said to me, 'Right, where's the bills? Electric bill, any bills you have, we want them, we're paying for them'. I could never have said a word about the UDA. They looked after me and my kids when Button Hill, their dad, was inside.

And the women were the first human barricade. We demonstrated against the soldiers in East Belfast to release our internees, our prisoners. We all went down, and we were standing outside the avenue, and the soldiers were standing down a good wee bit from us, and they kept shouting, 'if you'se are going do it, would you hurry up and get out!' So I walked out first and a whole crowd walked out behind me. And word had come to us that the Woodstock Road was out and had been barricaded too. They were barricading other roads, Beersbridge, everywhere had started to come out. Just women, no men. I was in the paper that night. One of the reporters came to me and I said, 'it's about our husbands being in prison, and they've not been charged with anything and they should be out'. And he says, 'who do you blame for that?' I must have said Billy Whitelaw. When I got home someone brought the paper in and it said, 'Mrs. Hill accuses Secretary of State William Whitelaw of ..' I forget what the word was, but I more or less accused him of interning our men. He was Secretary of State at the time so he must have made the decision.

58 We have had some tragedies
Geraldine Crawford

I was shot by the British Army when I was eighteen. It was October 1973. I was arrested and charged with possession of weapons in October 1973. Because of my injuries I spent over three months in Musgrave Park Hospital in the Security wing. Then in January 1974 I was moved to Armagh Jail. When I was in Armagh my sister Laura Crawford died along with Paul Fox in December 1975 as a result of an accidental explosion. They were both volunteers in the IRA. I was allowed out of Armagh for Laura's funeral and I walked alongside her coffin as a guard of honour.

I was released in October 1977 and went to work for the Falls Taxi Association. I remember I was interviewed by Leo Martin who was on the committee at the time. I started work in the Westside Service Station which was also a repair garage. It was next to the Lake Glen Hotel which was there at the time. Joe Clarke was the manager of the garage at the time and Bobby Storey senior was the chair of the committee. I worked between the garage and the Falls Taxi office which was facing Milltown Cemetery. At that time the prison protests were going on. There were other people employed by the Association then and we did quite a lot of work on behalf of the prisoners, photocopying and faxing material across the world. We moved from West Side Service Station over to where the car park is near the Job Centre at the Kennedy Centre. And at that time also we established a new private taxi firm, the Downtown Taxis, which also supplied limousines for weddings. We used to be brought home on a Friday afternoon in a limo when they were brought out to be cleaned and prepared for a Saturday wedding.

I was arrested again along with others at the funeral of Joe Mc Donnell who died on hunger strike in July 1981. I got out on bail in 1982 and was re-employed by Jim Neeson who was the general manager of the Taxi Association then. I was sentenced to another 8 years and got released in 1986 and got employed again in the taxi parts department alongside the office in Conway Mill. We were raided constantly by the police. They often took complete filing cabinets away to Castlereagh interrogation centre, and held them there for a few months. On one occasion all the staff had to present themselves at Woodbourne for interrogation by the C13 squad. We have had some tragedies throughout my years in employment. Eight drivers were shot dead while out driving and serving their community and others were murdered in their homes – just for being a Falls Road taxi driver. A few others were shot and wounded in the rank at Castle Street. But the service never failed the people of west and north Belfast and it has been a privilege and a pleasure to work alongside them for all these years.

59 Everything changed when I was eight years of age
Alan McVeigh

My father was a Brigadier in the UDA. When I was four and five years of age you'd have walked down into Ballybeen Square and he was there with his uniform on, and they were practicing their drills and everything else. And at that time it wasn't strange, because they were there with their combat jackets on and their hats and it seemed a normal thing. I remember in the general workers' strike we would get into the lorry and go and deliver. We went down to the farm and collected milk and eggs, and then there would be bread and potatoes, and we'd drive around Ballybeen delivering them. And I remember a couple of times being in his car and, obviously, they had road blocks up, and when we got to the road blocks he put his car window down and spoke to somebody, and we were allowed to go through. To me then it was all just part of growing up. It was natural, because you didn't know any other way. Everything changed when I was eight years of age. My father was murdered.

It was strange because you just went to school one day and came back and then… because he wasn't actually murdered there and then, they were kidnapped by the UVF, him and his helper, David Douglas, and then it was a lot of months before the bodies were found, so it was sort of… I remember thinking maybe, you know, he's gone on holiday or…

My mother was from a very close knit family of sisters and they were constantly at the house. My da was from a family of eleven or twelve, and then you had all these other men that you knew, you knew their faces, you knew that they were important in the estate. All these people coming to the house. It was months later their bodies were found in a shallow grave.

My father's family were all actually either policemen or well-to-do. They were a very Christian family. A lot of them never recovered from it. He has an eighty two year old brother, he lives in England, even when I meet him now he breaks down in tears because he was a serving officer in the RAF at the time so he wasn't allowed to come home for the funeral. My mother never recovered from it. I can remember she was taken to hospital, maybe three months after my father was eventually laid to rest, and the neighbours had to come in to look after us. Now we know that she'd had a nervous breakdown, that it had basically just knocked her for six. She could never tell me the details, and I would ask questions from older aunts and all but you were always shielded away from it. Our mother didn't want to tell us the full story behind it. But four years ago, at the age of forty two, I was contacted by the Historical Enquiries Team, and it was only then that I actually started finding out what had happened, how it happened, who did it. Still to this day, I don't know why they did it.

I think, if I'd have been older, I would have taken a whole different career path, because I think I would have automatically got dragged into paramilitaries. But as an eight year-old kid I just grew up angry with everybody.

60 **Who had broken the chain?**
Kieran Devlin

We used to have eight people in our taxis then. You had two in the front and then six in the back. A wee box there in the middle. And there were times, I can remember, when there was 13 in my taxi, going right up to Twinbrook. The Brits used to come down and close the barrier and wouldn't let us through to go down to get the people from Castle Street. I remember we used to break the chain, pull the barrier across, and let all the drivers go down. And I remember this one night when Sonny Reilly broke the chain, but I got scooped for it. And they brought me into the Saracen and brought me round onto the Shankill. They threatened to throw me out beside these guys all outside drinking at one of the bars. And then they brought me round the top end and down the Springfield and into Springfield Barracks. So they were questioning me there, 'Who had broken the chain?' and all that, and then they decided, 'Right away you go'. I said 'I'm not going anywhere. You bring me down to where you got me'. And they said, 'We can't get out'. I said, 'What do you mean, you can't get out?' They said, 'All your drivers are outside blowing the horns'. The taxis had blocked the road and they wouldn't let anybody out. Flashing lights and blowing their horns. Protesting to get me out.

61 **I don't think they ever got over it**
Eddie Kinner

In 1975 I volunteered for a bombing operation and the bomb went off early. Because of our injuries we were brought to the hospital. They realised who we were and we were arrested. The impact on the family was devastating. Being blown up, and how I was arrested, it was totally shocking. I think it had a major impact on both of my parents' health. It led to their early deaths. I don't think they ever got over it. Also the impact on my brothers and sisters. Whenever I got out one of my brothers sat down and told me how much he hated it, because all the attention focused around me being in jail. He was saying this to me at a stage where he had worked it through, because at that stage I was out of jail and he'd seen what I'd achieved quickly on my release. I was sentenced in December and it impacted on my family so much that they had no food for Christmas. What they had was packets of custard creams. They were only kids, they were primary school kids, and that was their Christmas while I was in jail. Yet I was getting parcels with things. In your initial imprisonment you were making demands, asking for things. Initially, when you started, you wanted the maximum permitted in the weekly parcel, and you expected the maximum. You weren't contemplating the burden you were putting on your parents and the rest of your family. You didn't realise what you were doing. When I eventually realised it I started to draw things back and was trying to reduce the size of my parcels. My parents, on the other hand, were comparing their parcels to other prisoners' parcels and they thought that they weren't providing enough for me and they were under pressure to build the parcels back up. It was only afterwards when we were talking about it that they're starting to say, 'whenever you wanted the parcel reduced we were embarrassed putting your parcel on the bus beside somebody else's. We're not providing the same.'

62 **An Ghaeilge agus streachailt pholaitiúil**
Gearóid Ó Cairealláin

Bhí dlúthbhaint idir an Ghaeilge in ár n-intinn agus an athrú polaitiúil, mar bhí múinteoirí againn a raibh dearcadh iontach náisiúnach acu. Is cuimhin liom, bhí bronnadh fáinne ann lá amháin agus an fear a bhí ag bronadh na bhfáinní ná Jimmy Drumm, fear as Conamara a tharla a bhí i Sinn Féin san am. Agus is cuimhin liom san óráid a thug sé, labhair sé i nGaeilge, ansin bhris sé i mBéarla, dúirt sé, 'if you learn Irish, we'll get rid of the Brits'. Bhí an dearcadh sin ionainn ón tús, agus bhí sé maith, sna blianta sin mar bhí saighdiúirí Shasana ag siúl thart, achan uile bhomaite d'achan lá, ag cur isteach ar dhaoine, ag cur isteach ar na cluichí peile, bhí imtheorannú ar bun. Ní raibh mé crua go leor le bheith i mo shaighdiúir agus ní raibh a fhios agam riamh cad é an bealach le clárú leis na hÓglaigh ach dhírigh mise ar m'aisling, an Ghaeilge a fhoghlaim agus pobal Gaeilge a thógáil thart timpill mar sin buille s'againne, ag neartú an chultúir agus na teanga agus ag iarraidh frithbhuille a dhéanamh in éadan an impiriúlachais chultúir seo a brúdh orainn leis na céadta bliain. Ó bhí mé ar scoil, shíl mise gur chuid den streachailt amháin a bhí ann, gnéithe éagsúla den streachailt amháin, furasta agamsa sin a rá, fuair mise an taobh is éasca dó, ach thuig mé, agus tuigim inniu gur cuid den streachailt amháin é.

The Irish language and political struggle
Gearóid Ó Caireálláin

There's a close connection between the Irish language in our minds and political change, because we had teachers with a strongly nationalist outlook. I remember there was a fáinne presentation one day and the man presenting the fáinnes was Jimmy Drumm, a Conamara man who happened to be in Sinn Féin at the time. And I remember the speech he gave, he spoke in Irish, and then he broke into English, he said, 'If you learn Irish, we'll get rid of the Brits.' We had that view from the start, and it was good because English soldiers were walking around, every single minute of every day, giving people a hard time, interfering with football games. Internment was underway. I wasn't hard enough to be a soldier and I never knew how to sign up for the IRA but I focused on my vision, to learn Irish and to build an Irish language community around the place because that was my blow, strengthening the culture and language wanted to counter this cultural imperialism that had been imposed on us for hundreds of years. From when I was in school, I thought it was part of the one struggle, different aspects of the one struggle. That's easy for me to say, I got the easiest part of it, but I understood and I understand today that it's part of the one struggle.

63 **The mist rolled away**
May Paul

I am and always will be so proud to have been one of the peace people. We wanted the world to see, 'No, we're not all bad. This is only the few'. And it did work, people did learn that. It was good fun, and it was a day out every Saturday. Our banner said, 'Ardoyne and Mountain View Wants Peace'. And, from Mountain View and Ardoyne, we all became friends. And if I'd been in the shop and somebody heard me speaking they'd have said, 'that's Sister Annie that carries the banner.' They all made good fun of that. But it was serious to us. We went every Saturday and booked the buses, and we must have went to every outlying town right round the north of Ireland. In fact one time we went down and we were meeting with our Catholic counterparts from the south of Ireland at a new bridge near Dundalk, and it was such an emotional day. Because it was such a heavy mist you couldn't see anything. And as we all started to cross the bridge it was as if somebody had rolled that mist away. It completely cleared as we met in the middle of that bridge. It was so emotional and such happy times. Just meeting all these people, and hugging people that you had never seen and you might never see again. But that's how strong the peace movement was. We really were out for peace. Nothing else.

64 **It's about time we used our heads instead of our fists**
David Colvin

I was eighteen when I was arrested and convicted of a number of charges, and I did seven years. The first couple of years were hard because there was a lot of disruption within the prison itself, and there was a lot of fighting going on. I lost a lot of remission for fighting with republicans. But then it just came to me, 'there must be something better than this'. So when I eventually got released I took an interest in community work. Because I'd time to reflect, when I was in jail, on what was happening on the outside. When I was on the outside you know, it was a way of life, it was just it, you done it. But when I was inside I was actually seeing ….you know, there was a lot of misrepresentation and misleading from politicians at the time, and a lot of people felt the same way and just said, 'There must be something better than this. If we're going to fight it's about time we used our heads instead of our fists'.

65 **Political thinking**
Jake Kane

I was involved at a very early age. I was sixteen years old and I was arrested and brought into the Crumlin Road. Eventually I went to Long Kesh and served my time in Gusty Spence's compound, Compound 21. It was somewhat surreal when I first went in through the gates of Long Kesh. It was very, very, dark, rolls of razor wire, watch towers and dogs so it had the feel of a prisoner of war camp with the old army Nissan huts, and then the structure of the UVF. There was a very strict regime. Gusty had us very disciplined. There was lots of education and we were encouraged to do sport to keep fit. I spent six years in Long Kesh and at that time we were granted special category status. But it was a hard time when my father died of cancer. It put an awful lot of strain on my mother coming up when I first heard my father had cancer. He only lived for about five weeks. In a short period of time he was dead. It was hard for me knowing I'm not going out to see my father when I got released. I came through it with the help of my friends within the compound structure and also family members helping me to get through it. And that happened with quite a lot of people within the compounds. I met an awful lot of nice fellas who were arrested from the streets of the Shankill and Woodvale areas, and also a lot of people from country areas. A lot of political discussions went on in the compounds, and a lot of people acquired high standards of education, and I've come to the conclusion that it definitely was the early stages of political thinking and was instrumental in the peace process of today with a lot of the thinking that Gusty got out of people. So a lot of compound men are very pro-active in community groups today.

66 **An chéad lá i bpríosún**
Seán Mag Uidhir

Fán am a bhain mé Bóthar Chromghlinne amach, bíonn tú trína chéile. Bhuail muid le beirt as Beechmount an mhaidin sin, Rick Sadler agus Gerard Davy. Agus, bhí súil caillte ag Rick Sadler, pléascán i Nansen Street trí seachtaine roimhe sin nuair a maraíodh óglach darbh ainm Stew Bailey sa phléascán. Ní raibh aithne againn ar na daoine sin agus bhuail sna cillíní faoin cúirt mar bhí na cillíní thíos ansin faoin chúirt in Townhall Street. Agus bhí fear a amháin a raibh a sciathán briste. Duine acu; sciathán briste. Duine; gan súil!

Bhí na bardaigh ag cur an uisce isteach san fholcadán agus uisce té amháin a bhí an duine ag cur isteach, ní raibh smacht againne ar an uisce. Agus bhí mise i ndiaidh léamh tamall roimhe sin fán Birmingham 6 agus iad ag gabháil isteach go Winson Green gur chaith siad isteach iad in uisce a bhí té ar fad. So, bhí sórt faoiseamh orm nuair a chonaic mé an t-uisce fuar ag gabháil isteach! Mar, is dócha leis an tsamhlaíocht bhí tú ag smaoineamh, 'an bhfuil siad ag gabháil muid a chaitheamh isteach i bhfolcadán té?'

Ach bhí sé maith go leor fán am a bhain muid sciathán A amach mar bhí daoine eile as Ard Eoin ar an sciathán; Bik McFarlane, Peter Hamilton agus Séamus Clarke. Daoine a raibh aithne againn orthu agus go láithreach fuair siad tae, caife dúinn, bainne, leabharthaí, raidió don oíche. Rudaí den sórt sin go dtí go bhfaighfeá stuif ó do chlann féin. Bhí tú i measc comrádaithe ansin agus bhí mothú maith thart fán ait.

The first day in prison
Seán Mag Uidhir

By the time I arrived at Crumlin Road, you're mixed up. We met two people from Beechmount that morning, Rick Sadler and Gerard Davy. Rick Sadler had lost an eye in an explosion in Nansen Street three weeks earlier, where another volunteer named Stew Bailey was killed. We didn't know those people and we met in the cells under the court because the cells were downstairs there under the court in Townhall Street. And there was one man with a broken arm. One of them – broken arm. One of them – no eye! The warders were pouring the water into the bath and the man was only putting in hot water, we had no control of the water. And I had read before that about the Birmingham Six going into Winson Green, that they threw them into water that was roasting. So I was kind of relieved when I saw the cold water going in! Because of your imagination, you began thinking, 'Are they going to throw me into a hot bath?' But it was okay by the time we reached A Wing because there were others from Ardoyne there: Bik McFarlane, Peter Hamilton and Séamus Clarke. People I knew, and they immediately got tea and coffee for us, milk, books, a radio for the night. That sort of thing until you got stuff from your own family. You were among comrades there and there was a good feeling around the place.

67 **That's where the peace process started**
Eddie Kinner

I was detained on the Secretary of State's Pleasure (SOSP) because I was only 17. Because I was an SOSP I didn't get special category status granted right away, I had to apply for it. Eventually I was transferred down to Long Kesh, Compound 21, and because I had been blown up and had injuries I was excused drill. The UVF compounds in Long Kesh were run on a strict military regime, where they drilled regularly, exercised regularly, kept the place spotless. You had a muster parade in full UVF dress every Monday. Sometimes Gusty would come out and everybody was shit scared of him. For me there are crucial elements of the prison experience that I think are instrumental to the peace process. When I first went into prison most people were on a war footing and they would have attacked each other. Loyalists and Republicans would have attacked each other. When you went down into Long Kesh you came in under Gusty Spence's command, and he had established a strict 'no first strike' policy. You were not allowed to attack other prisoners. Do not let the authorities try to use you to get something on Republicans and vice versa, because you're going to suffer the same as them. He had established a kind of council in which the command staff of the different paramilitaries would have met and cooperated in trying to improve the prison conditions for everybody, and they would have developed their different strategies in trying to do that. The camp council established a level of cooperation recognising that you were all in under the same disadvantage, and you were all being penalised. It's the same thing on the outside really. But I think that the one thing you had in common was that you were all prisoners, so you had to try to cooperate under those conditions. It was about trying to identify what you had in common and that allowed us to start cooperating with each other, seeing each other as human beings rather than as the enemy. We knew that if something could be achieved to improve the conditions that they would benefit from it and vice versa. For me that's where the peace process began and Gusty started setting that up.

68 **Boolavogue**
Susie Vallely

I ended up in jail in February 1976. We were out on an operation and a volunteer was shot dead, another volunteer got away, and me and another volunteer got arrested. I was then sentenced to seven years. The thing about it was we were caught on the 15th of February, so Liam and I were actually the last people to be charged before political status ended. Status ended on 1st March. I was twenty. You always kind of knew you were either going to go to jail or you were going to be killed. When I went in I saw all the faces I knew and I was sharing a cell with Marie Vallely (no relation). And Marie was like a mother hen to me, she really looked after me. Especially the first weeks, because it was very traumatic the way that I was arrested. But there were so many girls in the same boat so you just got on with it. Only that I felt a bit of a burden on my family, other than that I had no responsibilities, and there was great, great, support. I remember one time there was a folk group came into play and they gave me a tin whistle and they gave me a wee book. So I decided to learn that song Boolavogue. So I was practicing and practicing and all I heard was, 'would you for F's sake shut up, you and that tin whistle'. But I stuck with it and stuck with it. So this day I was sitting out in the yard on my own and I started to play it, and I played it right through and then I just stopped, and the next thing all I heard was cheering and clapping from all the wings. That was a nice thing, that's something that I always remember.

69 **Trevor was dead and I was three months pregnant**
Margaret Smith

When I was fourteen I used to run about with these girls and we used to go to Alexander Park and all over and they knew this group of fellas and one of them was called Trevor McNulty.

I was amazed because my Daddy came from the Free State and I thought we were the only McNultys in Northern Ireland. So we met each other and we went out together for a year, you know, young love. And after a year, I got fed up. I was coming into fifteen and I was leaving school and I was going to get a job and we finished. So I was working in Gallaghers about a year and I met this girl who also came from Ardoyne and she happened to mention that she knew Trevor. And through her he made a date with me. It was two years after we'd fell out and we met up again and I remember meeting him outside the GPO in Royal Avenue and we went to the pictures. Don't ask me what the film was because I don't know, we talked that much. And we were going together and that was in 1968. In February 1969 he asked me to marry him. I was seventeen and a half. We got engaged on July 11th 1969 and we were going to save up for two years before we got married. And then all hell broke loose in August 1969 and the Troubles started here and one of the main things was, there was a split in the republican sector. But we got married in '71. I became more involved then in politics because I knew more. Trevor had been involved with the Northern Ireland Civil Rights movement. He was very politically aware even at a young age, because his father was very politically aware. Trevor would have been very socialist, communist.

So we were involved with the Republican Clubs which used to be known as Sinn Fein. It was Official Sinn Fein. We used to sell papers, leaflets. We were very active in community work, in dealing with what was needed in the community. I mean, our war cry for years and years and years was, 'It's not the border, or what colour of flag or what colour of post box you have, it's the bread on your table and what job you have and what income you have coming in and the type of house you're living in, the type of education your child's getting and the type of medical care'.

At that particular time, this big split between the Official and the Provisional IRA was bad. There was people shot over it and there was always agitation between the two groups. Anytime stuff happened they had to bring in mediators in to defuse the situation. You'd have had older IRA men who had a bit of sense and you had priests; they brought them all in to mediate and stop the trouble and at this time July 1977 the mediators were brought in and the trouble was stopped. Everything was put a stop to. I was three months pregnant again. Sean was a year and a week old. My sister Mary was living with me at the time, and she was pregnant. That morning she took pains and me and my friend took her to hospital. We brought Mary up to hospital and she was admitted. And then we came back and we got out of a taxi in North Queen Street and I saw this guy running round the corner, one of our people and I said, "What wrong?" and he said, 'They're only after opening up on Bucky and Trevor.' So I ran up. Trevor and my brother-in-law were lying on the ground. Trevor, the blood was just coming out of his mouth. Joe, there was a big pool of blood around him. And that day the place was empty. It was a summer's afternoon, 27th July. Trevor was shot dead. Joe was injured. There were kids playing on the landing and the kids saw them searching him. They shot him three times in the back and when he was lying on the ground they put a bullet behind his ear and a bullet in the nape of his neck. So Trevor was dead and he got buried, and I was three months pregnant and I had young Trevor in January.

70 **Coal driving - one taxi, two drivers**
Seamus Rice

There really was nothing on and you couldn't go outside the district in that particular period. There wasn't much work in our part of the road, and the Troubles were happening. It was an experience to me, I wasn't familiar with a black taxi and it was a different world altogether.
I put my name down as a 'coal driver' in those days. That means one taxi, two drivers. Pat Shannon was the other one. There are not many now would have been 'coal driving'. The taxi would have been driven by one driver during the day and one driver at night. I worked during the day and got home at 6, half 6, or 7. Then, if nobody else worked it at night, I just worked on for a couple of hours. We had what you called the BMC taxis and the oil was flying out of it. When you went up the Whiterock you wouldn't get down it with the smoke! If you had 2 in the front and 6 in the back you did well to get up to the top of the Whiterock.

71 **Her word was law**
Ann Stevenson

I remember the brothers all joining up one time, joined up with the UDA. And they came in as proud as punch to tell my Mummy and Daddy, and she had her coat on and bang, down to some club, wherever it was, and she went in and she said, 'I'm afraid they won't be joining', and that was the end of that. My brothers would have been maybe 15, 16. All their friends were doing it, they had to do it. But my Mummy had different thoughts for them. 'So and so joined and my wee mate joined', and, 'I don't care who joined up, you will not be joining up.' She went down and faced them all. She wasn't letting them join anything. I think they sulked for a while, they weren't too happy, but Mother's word was law, her word was law. My Mummy used to say, 'the big lads are sending all the wee boys out to do their work, you will not be involved'.

72 **Thinking twice about pensioners**
Owen Doherty

There were loads of funny cases. I lifted a woman and she was actually, to tell you the god's truth, she looked like Miss Marple. With her wee hat, matching skirt and coat, and her wee handbag and her walking thing. And she said to me, 'what do I owe you?' And I said to her, 'you're a pensioner, 15p.' And she said right out, these other guys started laughing, I was afraid to laugh, 'who the …..give you that right to call me a pensioner.' And I said, 'darling, I'm not doing anything wrong. I'm calling you a pensioner because it will maybe save you a few shillings of the fare for you.' 'There you go again, calling me a pensioner.' She threw the money at me. This woman from the back shouts in, 'you'll not call that lady a pensioner again, will you?' I says, 'no way will I call her a pensioner.'

73 **An bomaite is ísle agam**
Jake Mac Siacais

Togadh muid ón bhloc sin go bloc folamh a bhí salach agus bhí uisce ar urlár. Agus tugadh greadadh dúinne mar is gnáth ach caitheadh muid isteach i gcillín… an cillín ina raibh mise, bhí sé lán uisce, ní raibh fuinneog ann agus bhí an geimhreadh sin iontach fuar. Ní raibh sé comh fuar leis an cheann i '78, ach bhí sé fuar i mí Eanáir. Agus fágadh muid ansin. Seo thart fá deich a' cloig san oíche agus fágadh muid ansin go dtí an maidín dár gcionn agus bhí sé comh fuair sin, agus bhí mé in ísle brí cibé. Ní raibh pluid nó blaincéad nó rud ar bith againn. Bhí muid lomnocht sa chillín fliuch seo. Agus mhair muid fríd an oíche ag rá, 'caithfidh siad na héadaí isteach chugainn' ag a seacht a chlog, níor chuir siad. Agus chuaigh siad isteach san iarnóin dár gcionn agus ansin dúirt mé, 'beidh an dinnéar ag teacht, ar a laghad gheobhaidh muid rud éigin té. Agus, ní dhearna muid aon ghearán. Cibé rud a rinne na bardaigh, glac muid leis. Agus tháinig an bardach chuig doras s'agamsa agus bhí na lads i ndiaidh scairteadh amach go raibh sceallóga agus corn beef againn don dinnéar. Ach nuair a tháinig sé chuig mo dhoras ní raibh ann ach píosa amháin corn beef. Agus d'amharc mé air, bhí mé chóir a bheith ag caoineadh. D'amharc mé ar an dinnéar agus d'amharc an bardach orm agus dúirt sé, 'don't look so dissappointed, there's two chips under it'. Agus shuigh mé agus dúirt mé, 'tá mé briste'. Bhí mé comh fuar sin agus in ísle brí agus thuig mé, 'Seo é. Beir greim ort féin. Caithfidh muid leanstan ar aghaidh anseo nó beidh daoine ag fail bháis.'

My lowest moment
Jake Mac Siacais

We were taken from that [H-]block to an empty block, which was dirty and the floor was wet. We were given a beating as usual but we were thrown into cells… the cell I was in was full of water, it had no windows and that winter was very cold. It wasn't as cold as the one in 78', but it was cold in January. And we were left there. This was around ten o'clock at night and we were left there until the next morning and it was so cold, and I was feeling down anyway. We had no sheets or blankets or anything. We were naked in this wet cell. And we got though the night saying, 'They'll throw the clothes in to us' at 7 o'clock, but they didn't. And they went in the following afternoon and then I said, 'Dinner will be coming, at least we'll get something warm.' And we didn't complain at all. Whatever the screws did, we took it. And the screw came to my door and the lads had been shouting out that we were getting chips and corn beef for dinner. But when he came to my door there was only one piece of corn beef. And I looked at him, I was nearly crying. I looked at the dinner and the screw looked at me and he said, 'Don't look so disappointed, there's two chips under it.' And I sat and said, 'I'm broken.' I was so cold and downhearted and I realised, 'This is it. Catch a grip of yourself. We have to keep going here or people are going to die.'

74 **61 SOSPs**
William Mitchell

So in March of 1974, whilst still at school at 15, I joined the junior wing of the UVF, the Young Citizen Volunteers. I couldn't name one specific incident that motivated me. It was what was going on around me. Indiscriminate attacks on my community. Some people I'd known that had been killed. I was arrested three weeks after my seventeenth birthday for a murder that I carried out when I was sixteen. I was arrested and convicted in June 1975, and because I was under 18 I was sentenced to be detained at the pleasure of the Secretary of State. It's another way of giving a life sentence to someone who is under eighteen.
And the way my mother found out about

it was when the army and police were raiding the house. It was devastating to her. Even now I can't bring myself to have the conversation with her, what her life has been like. Because I know I've hurt her so much. And you wouldn't know it from her, you know, nothing's changed. She's still the loving mother. But it totally devastated her life. So much so that she was on medication. She had to retire early. She had worked all her days for standard telephones which is now Nortel, and she was outstanding at her job apparently. She ran what's called a relay adjusting assembly line where they made phones. They sent her to Portugal to train their staff in Portugal. This is how good she was at her job. She had to leave all that. She had to move house because it was in the media. My name, my address, my photo. It just totally turned her world upside down. And she had a three year old at the time too, my kid brother. So she was trying to manage all this, and then she's having to run up and down to Long Kesh prison camp for the next thirteen years. She became involved in campaigning. I think over the history of our conflict there have been 61 SOSPs. Secretary of State's Pleasure prisoners. At that time within the UVF and UDA there was about 10 or so, and they formed this family group to campaign about the treatment of underage prisoners. That campaign was not that successful, but it raised the profile of the plight of young political prisoners. My mother is a devout religious person and after my arrest, you know, her life was in ruins. And in spite of my father being an atheist he's one of the most Christian men I have ever known. His views, his principles, his respect for others. So I had that upbringing within the house.

75 **i mbun léachta...**
Seán Mag Uidhir

Leabhar a scríobh Kitson ag an am ná *Bunch of Five*, nuair a bhí sé ag cur síos ar streachailtí ar fud an domhain a bhí sé páirteach ann; Malaysia agus áiteanna eile. Rinne muid léachtaí air agus bhí muid ag plé Malaysia agus an rud a rinne siad leis na treallchogaithe Síneacha ansin - Bhog siad an ghnáthmhuintir ón áit a raibh siad lonnaithe go dtí oileán éigin eile ar fad agus d'fhag siad na treallchogaithe ina n-aonar, sa jungle. Bhris siad an nasc idir na treallchogaithe agus an pobal. Bhí Brendan Curran as Lorgan i mbun na léachta seo agus bhí sé ag rá ag an deireadh, 'bhuel, cad é a d'fhoghlaim sibh as an léacht sin?' agus ar ndóighe bhí sé fanacht ar fhreagra den sórt, 'bhuel, caithfidh tú an nasc a choineáil idir na trodairí agus an pobal' agus a leithéid sin. Agus cara de mo chuid as Clonard, dúirt sé, 'stay out of the jungle!'

Giving a lecture...
Seán Mag Uidhir

'Bunch of Five' was a book written by Kitson at the time, where he described struggles around the world in which he was involved, Malaysia and other places. We did lectures about it and we discussed Malaysia and what they did to the Chinese guerrillas there – they moved the general population from the area where they were based to some other island and left the guerrillas alone, in the jungle. They broke the link between guerrillas and the people. Brendan Curran from Lurgan was giving this lecture and he was saying at the end, 'Well what did you learn from that lecture?' and of course he was waiting for an answer like, 'Well, you have to keep the link between the fighters and the people' and that sort. And a friend of mine from Clonard said, 'Stay out of the jungle!'

76 **The community also served us**
Sean Carmichael

We had great support from people that used us. People knew that they were as much a target as we were but they weren't deterred. They were apprehensive, probably fearful like everybody else. But just as I say the black taxis were serving the community, the community also served us. The community backed us up. I wasn't a driver at the time Hugh McGee was murdered but I knew the two people, Mrs Russell and somebody else, that was in his motor, and after Hugh was murdered they continued to use us. Hugh was shot once at the corner of Rosapenna and then his motor went out of control, the gunman ran across the road and then finished him off and they were in the back of the motor. And they still used us. There was a wee woman from the Bone called Sue Slavins, and she's dead now, God rest her, and she was in Joe Devlin's motor when Joe Devlin's motor was attacked. Joe came up to the corner of Rosapenna which is at the corner of the Oldpark Road. The windscreen was smashed but lucky enough nobody was injured, Joe and everybody was safe. And Sue said to one of our drivers, she wasn't going to use them again, but then within so many minutes she went, 'No, no, no. These people aren't beating me'.

77 **White socks**
Ally Kennedy

I can remember hearing that if you wear white socks they would know you were a Protestant. And I remember I was in a car accident when I was sixteen. My face was all cut open and I had to go to the Falls Road to the Royal, and I said to the ambulance man, 'Where are we going?' He said, 'The Royal,' and I said, 'Where is that?' He said 'Falls Road,' and I got myself in such a panic because I knew I was going to the Falls Road, and I remember looking down to see if I was wearing the white socks. I was so scared, the fear was unbelievable. Even when they were stitching my face up, I was so conscious, terrified, because I knew I was on the Falls Road, in the hospital.

78 **Starting the no wash protest as a prisoner in Armagh Gaol**
Breige Brownlee

Eight years in jail, there was times when it was harsh. I spent my 21st birthday on the no-wash protest, it was hard, it was disgusting and it was dirty. My first experience….when it happened we were actually in cells, there was cell searches. It was a deliberate policy by the screws and the Brits to push us on to that because they wanted to break…..they thought the women in Armagh were the weak link. We didn't deliberately go out and say, 'we're going on the no-wash today'. They pushed us into a situation where there were no choices. And the first day….we would still have had stuff in our cells. We had clothes, we had books, we had make up, we had hair stuff, we had food on the windowsills. We were locked in the cells. They wouldn't let us out to go to the toilet, and this went on for hours and hours and hours and hours and hours, and I was the first person that had to go to the toilet, and I said 'oh god, I can't do this. I cannot do this'. But there was no choice. There really was no choice. Within a week, we were taken out, a cell at a time, through the tunnels from B wing to A wing. There's what's called a suicide wire within the prisons. They had boarded the suicide wire to separate the wings. They had stripped all the cells. All there was in the cells was two iron beds. Absolutely nothing else and they had actually put wooden boards across the windows. That was us for the duration. For the first months they didn't even move us out of cells so there was a build up of everything you can imagine. But I have to say, it was the best year of my life. Because when you are down to nothing, you only have each other and that's where the friendship, the comradeship, came in.

79   **Black clouds**
Michael Pike

I joined the Scots Guards and I finished my basic training in February /March 1981. The Scots Guards were based in Alexander Barracks near Aldergrove airport. And they would go and do two week stints in Belfast. The Markets, Ardoyne, Newlodge, Falls, Divis, Unity - all the republican areas. And of course the hunger strike kicked off at that time. So that meant we were in the city a lot more because they swamped Ireland, Northern Ireland, with British soldiers. The clock was ticking. Bobby Sands was on hunger strike for sixty-six days. We went on leave before he died and the tension was building. So I went on leave and I was doing the dishes at home and my dad came in and said, 'are you alright son?' And I said 'The shit's going to hit the fan Dad, I can't go back.' He said, 'Son you've got to go back. You cannot run away you know.' And of course I went back but that journey from Glasgow to Belfast was so depressing. It's a half hour drive from Milngavie to the airport. My brother was in the back of the car, my dad was driving. I couldn't even look at them. I'd look out the window. Black clouds. It was awful. But when you got to the airport and you saw a couple of the boys you began to loosen up a wee bit. Because we were all the same. You could see the big black clouds over everybody's heads as we were coming back from two weeks of madness, of spending loads of money and getting drunk. Back to reality, but this time the reality was different. Bobby Sands was dead.

Coming to Belfast I was in no way prepared for the level of hatred towards me. And I took that very personally. After my initial Northern Ireland training, which is separate from your basic training, I was sent out with a bunch of Fusiliers just to break me in gently. Well it wasn't gently at all. We were walking the streets. They pulled a car over. 'Right search the car.' So I'm like looking around and things and he said, 'no search it.' And this family, kids in the back, wife in the passenger seat, and the guy, and they were glaring at me. And they were pulling panels off doors, and into the boot and pulling up everything. And I've never done this before. And the looks I was getting from this woman and these kids and this man. I just did not enjoy that at all.

Very, very quickly you put your barriers up and you became as hate filled as they were towards us. They stopped being people to me. They were the enemy. They hated us. Kids, grannies, even dogs. You're not talking one or two. Massive communities, thousands of people, despised us. That was hard to take. I was expecting a few individuals. A few hundred. But half a million?

80 Those bin lids still echo in my head
Liz Groves

The hunger strikes were terribly, terribly … it is hard to explain. Anybody who didn't live through that, it is desperately hard to explain how you felt. How hurtful they were, how soul destroying it was. It is hard to describe, and it is still emotional, because we knew them. Joe and Kieran were particularly good friends. We were one of the few houses that had a telephone that people could feel free to come in and use. So we were one of the first phone calls to say that Bobby had died. We had been sitting up all that night anyway because we knew that it was very close. And those bin lids still echo in my head. And I know other people who felt the same, that every time they hear it, even on TV, that the flash backs are absolutely horrible. And how the Church reacted was a big insult to me personally. Now it's not that they did anything on me personally, but these were people whom I loved. These were people that I knew. These were people who were strong, strong, community based caring guys. Why would they give up their lives if they weren't strong, if they weren't caring, if they weren't all of that? And these priests were refusing them entrance to their church. They were refusing them the honours that they should have been given. Joe McDonnell's funeral completely sickened me. The priest from St Patrick's. I just thought, 'You bastard, you rotten, rotten, bastard, how dare you close the doors of that church. It is not yours'. It changed my whole attitude to religion. I tell our kids, 'God is not in a building'. And that day proved it, Joe McDonnell's funeral proved that god doesn't belong in a building, he belongs out there on the streets with his people.

81 We were ploughing a lonely furrow
Jim Watt

After I was sentenced I was brought down to the H Blocks, and the first thing is they would have taken all your clothes away and given you this prison uniform to wear. And I said, 'well I'm not wearing the uniform'. People know about the republican blanket protest which had already started but there were some loyalists engaged in the blanket protest as well. The blanket protest was a very enlightening thing because you got to know people that you basically regarded as your enemy and you would have hated, but because you were in a situation where you were being oppressed you formed a common bond. I remember one time we had all been moved down the punishment blocks. What happened about every 10 days was they had to empty the wings and power hose it and clean it because of the excrement from the republicans who were on the dirty protest. So they had to find somewhere to put us while they were cleaning the wing. And we were put in the punishment block this time. And there was a number of republicans down, they were going to court. And a judgement had been brought out then that the prison was entitled to give them forced baths if they were going to court. And I remember the beating and the abuse and humiliation they got. I couldn't see it, I could only hear it all. And I remember us up at the doors shouting at the screws. Here are people that I flippin' hate but I'm supporting them. So it forced you to look at things and try and understand. I think it was a very good thing. I never changed my views. I'm still British and I'm still unionist. I don't feel Irish in any sense or form. But prison, at least, put me in a situation where I thought more about the greater picture of Northern Ireland.

I often say if the whole of the loyalist paramilitaries had taken part political status would have been achieved far earlier, at less cost, and without the hunger strikes. But, for various reasons, I feel that the loyalist blanket protest was undermined by people who had been placed in positions of authority within the UVF in the prison. For whatever reasons, they didn't want to take part in any protest or come into conflict with the authorities. So the UVF prisoners were not encouraged from within the command structure in the prison, whereas we would have received great support from the compounds and the likes of Gusty and that. So in many ways it was quite hard for the small group of loyalists. The republicans had a big mass of prisoners, and they had a propaganda machine, and they had the support outside. Whereas we were kind of ploughing a lonely furrow.

82 You needed somebody to do your time with
Jackie Upton

I was 19 when I was arrested. I always sort of wanted to do more. I'd seen the women going and standing and being at the corner blocking the roads, but they were only used for bits and pieces. So when I was approached to do something I didn't refuse – well if these people need the money for whatever reason well then I'll do what I have to do. I was taken to Mountpottinger police station and interviewed there for two days. They had told me that I wasn't arrested, that I was just going in for a talk to clarify a few things because they just had information received. It was a bit silly and naïve of me now I know. I had no solicitor nor was I given that information that you were entitled to a solicitor. And they told me you're not going to see your family, no visits because of what you've done, paramilitary organisation is not going to help you now, if you fill in this statement it will be far better for you. It was all psychological, and you're taking in all this information, and you're not used to being where you are. If I had never had made that statement I would never have got time, but looking back now, it was meant to happen. I've always said bigger men have made statements and went down for life. So I accept that now because I always regretted that for a long time. I ended up getting two years and I'd never been in trouble before in my life. I always remember being convicted of the two years. I was waiting on him saying the words, 'but I will suspend your sentence', and it never came.

And then we were brought to Armagh Gaol, and I was in the wing with about 30 odd republican prisoners and four Protestants including myself. They were ordinary prisoners. One got out on appeal, and the other two were getting out, so then I was left in the wing on my own with about 30 republican prisoners, including Mairead Farrell. I put the request in to get moved and I was just flatly refused. I now know I was used as a pawn in the system. Mairead approached me and wanted a plan because they wanted segregation obviously. And the plan was beating me up, with my co-operation, to help my case of getting off the wing. But beating me would have been a big risk because there was a screw with me at all times. And they had lost all their remission because of the dirty protest which they had just come off and scaled it all down. The system used me to keep them from getting segregation.

There was a screw with me at all times. I was escorted to the bathroom. I didn't do any classes in Armagh, it was just too intimidating. I mean you had 28 republicans all glaring at you, moving the seats or knocking you by as you walked past. The screw couldn't do anything because you were accidently hit or they wouldn't let you past, just stupid silly things that were just constant. It was just constant mental torture and very intimidating.

You needed somebody to do your time with. I was in that wing from end of June until September nearly on my own. I eventually wouldn't go out of my cell. I said, 'I'm not coming out while I'm on this wing on my own'. I wouldn't go to work and I says, 'if you don't move me I'm just staying in my cell, I'm not coming out, I'm just staying here because I don't feel safe. I don't want to be in this wing, I don't see any reason why you can't move me to B Wing so I'll just stay in this cell'. It obviously worked because in September they moved me. I was sentenced on the 18th May and it took to September. But when they moved me then some other innocent Protestant came in and took my place. B Wing was completely different. Doing the time with another person, even just if you didn't feel right that day, you just were down, you had somebody to talk to apart from the screw.

83 We were trying to do something to gain something
Jim Rea

Prison was hard, good days and bad days. It was hard without your wife and family and friends, but you just had to get on with it. I was in H2 in Magilligan at the time. I was in B wing and we had the majority of Protestants in our wing, there weren't too many Catholics. The Provies were in the majority over the Protestants in the other three wings, and they were beating the Protestants every day of the week. So we decided, enough is enough, we will do something about this. The top boys held a meeting in the church on a Sunday morning and came and informed us all that on Monday night, after TV, we were to get stuck into any Catholics that were in the canteen. So we beat the crap out of them, there was blood everywhere. Then after that Protestants were being treated badly so we decided enough is enough and started the dirty protest. This was in 1982. Throwing urine out the cell doors, and the decision was taken to put our excrement up over the walls. You got used to it. You had to do it and that was it. I remember my dad coming up to see me, and he walked past me because I had a bit of a beard and my hair was long, and I had to say, 'Dad where are you going'? And my da walked past me, because my beard was stinking and my hair long. Sometimes they would let you back into the canteen, but the majority of time we had to eat in the cells surrounded by excrement and urine. We were on the protests a few months. We would get switched, they would come in and put us in the clean cells, then clean the dirty cells, and we would be doing the same in the clean cells, then they would shift us back. They got other Protestant prisoners to clean the cells. There were prisoners who just couldn't handle it. I was bitter because it was mates you were doing time with and were knocking about with every day of the week, then a bit of hard time comes along and they can't hack it. We were trying to do something to gain something, and they were coming and cleaning the cells again. When we were on protest, if we weren't arguing with Republicans, if the Protestants lost all their privileges, the Republicans came along and handed tobacco and tea bags and whatever else, and if they lost all their privileges through protest, it was vice versa. You had to get on and support each other. At times we did get on. We had our ups and downs certainly, getting into fights with one and other, it was only to be expected. Even when we were on that protest we never saw politicians, but there were priests and all coming up to see Republicans. But never any politicians up to see us. Things haven't changed.

84 **Mister are we getting hijacked?**
Joe Burns

I was a driver first of all, and then I was a loader. How I left driving the taxis is that I was coming down from Andersonstown one time with a full load and I decided I was going home. So I pulled into the house with a full load. A full load of passengers all going home with me. And this woman in the front seat beside me said, 'Mister, are we getting hijacked?' I turned around and said, 'sorry love, no, it was in my mind I'm going home'. And that was it, I went onto the loading. I was on the committee and was asked to go on the loading.

85 **The following April**
Jude Whyte

Even 30 years later, those days are as clear as anything and they shouldn't be. We were a big family living in University Street on the edge of a Catholic area. The main protagonists weren't the police. I mean by and large the cops treated you with indifference. You were always tortured by the Ulster Defence Regiment on your way to school or on your way anywhere. There were three attacks on our house, two bomb blasts and an incident on the way. There was a death squad came to us in '83. The police actually intercepted them, shot one of them dead, arrested one of them, and one got away. Then in November '83 a bomber, David Maitland, was charged. He planted a bomb at the back of our house but it blew up prematurely. So I had the unenviable task, because my Ma told me, of going out and putting a pillow under this fellow's head. I'm not sorry I did it. I'm glad I did it. But the effect it's had on me, if I had of known, I might not have done it. Where you get this image coming back to you periodically, that sort of upsets you. And then the following April, a bomb was planted at the front of the house and it killed mammy and a young fella, a 23 year old guy called Michael Dawson, a policeman from Braniel. The guy who did that, I do understand the context. They believed, because they were being fed information by the UDR probably, or the police, that we were a republican family. We were a GAA family. I don't honestly know any real connection with the republican movement in any of my family. My father and mother were members of the Alliance Party and my Da was a great friend of a guy called David Cook who was the first non-unionist Lord Mayor of Belfast in the '80s and a great friend of a guy called Basil Glass who was another big wig in the Alliance Party. The only thing you'd get a dig in the face for, in our house, was if there was something on the TV and you made a sectarian comment. That's the only thing I can ever remember my Da losing the rag over.

86 Her first prison visit
Donna Spence

I knew Stephen was in the UDA when we got married. I was still very young. He got remanded in Crumlin Road jail. That was a whole culture shock. Having to run up to the jail three times a week. The expense of traveling up and down, getting him parcels and clothes. I was seven months pregnant and David was a year and a half. I gave birth to my daughter while he was still inside, so my daughter was nine days old when she had her first prison visit and it was heart breaking.

You had to try and cope on your own, but I must say, my mammy was very good. She looked after us, food wise and clothing the kids, plus mental strength as well. You had your weepy moments. It was hard but you had to do it because you stood by your man. Steven got out when she was 3 ½ months old.

87 Paddy McAllister was a lovely man
Breige Brownlee

I mean our drivers really were in the front line. They were because they were out there working no matter what happened, no matter what was going on, no matter whether there were bombs, bullets, whatever, our drivers worked this road. There has never been a day when there hasn't been black taxis working. At the worst of times the drivers actually would have done double shifts, triple shifts. They would have been there 24/7 if they were needed. When one of our drivers was shot or injured or killed it spread the whole way through the organisation. I'm thinking of one driver in particular, from my area, Paddy McAllister. Paddy was a lovely family man. To this day his wife is just heartbroken and his family are heartbroken. A lovely man shot dead in his own house and, you know, that ripples through everybody. And the passengers are as important as the drivers. A lot of the passengers get to know the drivers as well. So when our drivers were killed a lot of the passengers were very, very affected by it as well. There's people who would have got Paddy's taxi every morning going to work and it affected them as much as it did us. The ripples were unbelievable that came from that. But it never ever deterred drivers.

88 The Mars Bar Factory
Mark Anderson

My dad was inside but we didn't know what he was inside for. I do remember, at an early age, going into Belfast and getting on the bus and going up to the jail. But we were always told it was a Mars Bar Factory, believe it or not. A Mars Bar Factory, that was where my dad worked. You went through the doors and you go in, you sit down at a table and our dad would come out to us. I always remember the orange juice. We always got this wee cup of orange juice in a plastic cup and a Mars Bar, which is why we always thought we were going to the Mars Bar Factory. So the troubles and Northern Ireland to me wasn't something I knew about until early teenage years.

89 Sin an t-atmaisféar a bhí ann
Danny Brown

Bhí punk i ndiaidh tarlú i mBéal Feirste agus bhí suim mhillteanach agam sa cheol, bhí ariamh. Chonacthas domh, cé nach punk a bhí ionam ar chor ar bith, go raibh rud speisialta i ndiaidh tarlú i mBéal Feirste. Ní dheachaigh mé isteach don fhaisean nó rud ar bith, ach bhí an ceol… bhí brí agus fuinneamh ann agus tharraing sé daoine le chéile, is cuimhin liom sin ag na gigeanna. Ní raibh mé riamh chun tosaigh ag caitheamh seile le daoine! Ach chonacthas dom go raibh brí agus fuinneamh millteanach sa Harp Lounge. Ach chomh luath agus a d'fhág tú sin, bhí na Shankill Butchers… B'fhéidir go mbeadh go leor airgid agat i do phóca fágtha fá choinne black taxi, sin síos go dtí lár na cathrach. Ach ag siúl abhaile an chuid eile agus fan am a bhain tú barr an New Lodge Road amach bhí tú stuama, le heagla. Mar sin an t-atmaisféar a bhí ann.

That's the atmosphere that existed…
Danny Brown

Punk had arrived in Belfast and I had a massive interest in music, always have. I realised, although I wasn't a punk at all, that something special had happened in Belfast. I didn't go in for the fashion or anything, but the music was… it was full of vigour and energy and it pulled people together, I remember that at the gigs. I was never at the front spitting at people! But it seemed to me that there was a great energy in the Harp Lounge. But as soon as you left there, the Shankill Butchers were… You might have had enough money left in your pocket for a black taxi, down to the city centre. But walking home the rest of the way and by the time you reached the top of the New Lodge Road you were sober, with fear. Because that's the atmosphere that existed.

90 **You were there when nobody was there**
Paul Rooney

It's like comradeship or it's just a closeness, you know, people wanting to help each other because there was nobody else there to help the people of all these areas. The black taxis just came into it all and through the troubles. We've got pensioners now using the taxis and they don't have to use taxis because they've free travel. But they're determined. You'll stand out there and you'll see the pensioners coming in and they'll say, 'sure I wouldn't go in anything else, you were there when nobody was there'. And you know that there gives you a wee lift when you hear people.

91 **Me, Margaret, Jill, Loopy Lou and Mary**
Betty Morrison

When I was working in Boots there were five of us - me, Margaret, Jill, Loopy Lou and Mary - three Catholics and two Protestants. I was from the Shankill, Jill was from the Ormeau Road, Margaret was from Unity Flats and Loopy Lou, as we called her, Lucinda, her name was, she was from Andersonstown, and Mary was from the Falls. So we were all out on our lunch hour going round the town, gagging the way we did. And we were walking along Royal Avenue and the next thing these soldiers just pulled us in to the side. 'Where are you'se going?' And I said, 'We're out on our lunch hour, we're in our uniforms, can you not see? We work in Boots.' We were that embarrassed, everybody was going along and looking at us out in the street, and he searched our handbags and all the rest of it, and then he went, 'Name? Where are you from?' 'Betty Morrison, Shankill', and as I said,

'Andersonstown, Unity Flats, Ormeau Road and the Falls', he just looked at us all. And he said, 'Well how come you'se are all together from Catholic places and Protestant places?' And I said, 'Well, we work together and we've been working together for years, and we're good friends and we're out on our lunch hour'. And he couldn't get over that and then he let us go. We were still laughing when we got into work.

92 **A walking stick**
Paddy Mulvenna

It was hard and very difficult. There was one driver in particular; in fact he would have been a second cousin of mine. His mother and my mother were two full cousins. He was Harry Muldoon. He came over here one night and he sat on that settee there and he was saying to me, 'Paddy', he says, 'I feel my life's under threat here, you know, what can I do?' He was in the Star, a social club in Ardoyne, and he came out on to the front of the road at Twadell Avenue and he was chased by a group of men, but he happened to get away once he got down into Mountain View where he lived. He was a bit shook up about it. And I said, 'Harry you're going to have to tighten up your security. Cut out the Star at night time. If you want a wee drink, have it in the house. Fortify your front doors and back doors and all'. This was only a couple of weeks before Harry was shot dead. You couldn't have met a nicer fella. Quiet, you know. He adopted two girls, two lovely wee girls, and his wife died young. And he brought them up and they were in the house. He came running out at the top of the stairs and he had a walking stick. That was his security, a walking stick.

93 **My whole life changed**
Kay Spence

Billy was about six or seven years older than me and he had been in the Paras, but by the time I'd met him he'd come out of the army. We went to live in Foyle Street but Billy, unfortunately, got caught up with people that were involved, and because of his army background he was a very good recruit, if you want to put it in those terms. I was worried that Billy was getting in deeper and deeper but didn't realise to what extent he was getting involved. And, just literally, what he was willing to do. It came out whenever he was actually arrested. They had him for nearly a week questioning him, and I didn't know what was going on. I went to the organisation headquarters, the welfare department of it, the Eagle as it was known then, and I says, 'Look, I don't know what to do here'. And they said, 'if you go to the Presbyterian minister at the Woodvale, he'll maybe help you out'. And he says, 'Well, I'm willing to go up to Ladas Drive with you to help you to get in to see the detectives to see what's happening. I didn't get seeing Billy, but the detectives brought me in, and it ended up that they were questioning me to see what exactly I knew. But, because Billy had kept all those kind of things from me, I really wasn't really able to tell them anything. I was just a complete wreck when I found out what it was that he was…..because the detectives, when they were questioning me, said, 'Do you know that your husband shot a man down in front of his child and followed him up into his parlour and put five bullets into him?' I said, 'My husband wouldn't do that'. I says, 'He wouldn't. He couldn't'. Well by the time he'd come to court he'd changed his plea from not guilty to guilty. He was held in Crumlin

Road jail on remand so I went three times a week to see him, sometimes with the children, sometimes without the children. It depended on whether I could get them minded or not. When he was moved to Long Kesh it was a different kettle of fish altogether, because you left the Eagle at about eight, half eight, in the morning, in a minivan full with all prisoners' wives all going down to see their husbands, and you could have been not getting home to six or maybe eight o'clock that night. So it was a long day because, although you would have only got a half an hour's visit in Long Kesh, you had to wait on everybody else coming out from their visits. My whole life changed. I lived around going to Long Kesh and looking after my children and that was it. You couldn't really call it a life.

You went up and you visited them once a week for half an hour, and after six years I was still going up to Long Kesh with the children, and then I met someone else which was very difficult at that time because you were classed as a prisoner's wife. You weren't allowed to do anything. You had to be very careful because you were a prisoner's wife, so therefore you were watched everywhere you went. Everybody you spoke to, it was a quiz as to how you knew them. How long you knew them? What they were? What they weren't? Like even people, fellas that I'd went to school with, who weren't in any one way romantically linked to you, it was a question mark if you spoke to them. You know you were supposed to go around with, I think, blinkers on. So as I say, it was quite serious as regards Geordie, who is now my second husband, because they did phone and threaten to shoot him if he didn't stay away from Glencairn and stay away from the prisoner's wife and all. And that went on for quite a while. It was the hardest thing in my life that I had to do the day that I went up to Long Kesh to tell him that I wouldn't be back. It was terrible actually. And he just didn't want to believe it, couldn't believe it. And asked then would I come back up so that he could talk to me, and I said, 'Well, right, okay'. We'd been married ten years by this time. Married ten years and only together four, to be quite honest, whenever he was lifted. I was only twenty four whenever Billy was lifted so by this time I was coming up to thirty.

94 It came right to my door
Terry Lyons

During the height of the troubles the taxis were running the gauntlet of approximately four roadblocks a day. Two in the morning, two in the afternoon. There were some that were more aggressive, one unit in particular. They stopped me one day at Springfield corner as I came across the lights with a full load on and they said, 'get your passengers out', and I said 'no, that's not my job.' And he's telling me again, so I got out of the taxi and I opened the door and I said to my passengers, 'ladies and gentlemen, listen to these RUC men. They're harassing me. They want me to get you out of my taxi', and I said 'there's no reason for you to get out of the taxi', and one word led to another. So it ended up I appeared four times in court and I was fined £112 for harassment of the RUC.

In 1988 it came right to my door. I had a taxi ready for PSV sitting at my door and it was burnt at 11.45 at night. The neighbours described them shouting directions to each other in broad English accents getting away and they were in plain clothes. That came right to my door. But that was a vehicle that could be replaced. Life can't. And this is where

I feel it, from the point of view of my wife, my children, when I think of those other eight association members who were murdered. But all this actually bonded our community more than ever. Every atrocity carried out against the taxi association, got support from our people, and our people were supported by the black taxi association.

95   I was knocked back twenty years
Tommy Harrison

Two of my class mates in Summerdale were murdered in 1974, John Bailey and Joe Taylor. They were murdered within 5 days of each other. Joe Taylor had a job in the petrol station on the West Circular Road. They actually went into the petrol station and shot him dead. Joe was seventeen. John Bailey was a Christian and had a lot to do with the BB, the Boys Brigade. He'd been walking home with his father and his friend. They were probably coming from the church hall. It was a drive by shooting. They opened up. I think the three of them were hit. John was killed stone dead. And the talk then was going about that it's the same murder gang from the same area. I would say there was a lot of school mates went down the same road as I did, maybe to different paramilitaries. But these were two school friends that I know for definite didn't join any paramilitary organisation and they were never known for getting involved in any riots in the areas that they lived in. So those were bad days.

I was brought back then mentally to my school days at Summerdale when a few incidents happened, particularly one of the incidents, I was knocked back at least twenty years. My brother-in-law and my sister were both blown up by a booby-trap bomb under their car. My brother-in-law was killed instantly. My sister, I don't know how she survived, she was critically ill for months and has still never got over this mentally. They were going to the Chinese to bring back something to eat, and God only knows how they made a decision that night not to take the two kids out. They never got to the Chinese. As soon as they turned round the bend… it was a mercury tilt switch, apparently, and the car was blown to smithereens. So coming up towards the likes of the peace process and stuff, I was very, very sceptical because, in my mind, mentally, I was knocked back twenty years and I was very very angry then. That happened in 1988.

96   Joe's co-pilot
Stevie O Reilly

I became involved in the black taxis through my uncle, Joe Reid. Joe passed away two years ago. Joe used to get me to brush the back of the taxi every time he came in from work. It evolved from that. At that time the Troubles were at their height, there were soldiers on the street and rioting and stuff like that. Joe took me out in the taxi with him to keep me safe and off the street. So it evolved from there, going up and down the road, getting to know all the drivers, getting them tea in the old Castle Street. They used to call me Joe's co-pilot. My friends were getting into sports, GAA, soccer teams, BMX bikes and things like that, but I preferred to go out and sit in the front of the taxi travelling up and down the road. There was never any doubt in my mind. That's what I wanted to do.

97 My dad is gone, I am not going to see him again
Mark Anderson

In '92 my father was murdered. I would have been eight or nine. To a degree I knew there were troubles, but I didn't understand them. I remember actually the day it happened, I was at school and my headmaster came to my classroom and got me and my brother out of class and took us down to his office and my uncle was there. And my uncle said to me, 'There has been an accident'. I remember going, 'What kind of an accident?' And he said, 'Your dad is dead'. I didn't know what way to react. I don't think I believed it at first, until I got home. I got out to the house and my mother was in the next door neighbour's house and I went in and she said, 'Did your uncle tell you?' And I said, 'Yes', and she started crying and I started crying and my younger brother started crying. Then my older brother, he was maybe fifteen, he came in and he was crying. I sort of realised then he wasn't coming back. I had my family around me but it wasn't the same. I didn't have my da and I didn't have a father figure. I think more when I got into high school, I started to realise how much I actually missed my dad. Nine, ten years of age it was, my dad is gone, but when I got into high school, I realised he is gone; I am not going to see him again. Until this day, I think one of the hardest things for me is my son, who I named after my dad, is never going to get to see his granda and that really gets to me at times.

98 The people's taxis
Jim Neeson

The seven drivers that were killed during my time, there were three of them at least, were my friends, Paddy Clarke in particular. Paddy Clarke was the chairperson. The number of drivers that were killed and the number of drivers that were shot. There was an attack in Castle Street one night and there was nobody actually injured because the machine gun jammed. We had other drivers at Brown Square who were attacked. And the harassment the drivers got, and their passengers. Usually what they did was, they took the driver out, searched him, messed him about, but also put the passengers out onto the street. There was also this loyalty to the taxis. One of the things I always tell people about was driving up and down the road on a really wet wintry morning. And a bus would come along and there would be six, eight, ten people standing and they wouldn't get on the bus, they got on the taxi. They were the people's taxis, they were our taxis. And really and honestly, it was an experience for me that I just loved.

99 An bhfuil tú ag gabháil ar ais go príosún?
Seanna Breathnach

Rinne mé amach gan gabháil ar ais go príosún. Rugadh orm red handed faoi thrí, ní uair amháin nó dhá uair ach faoi thrí. Bhí a fhios agam nach dtiocfadh leo mé a bhriseadh agus mé faoi cheist. An dóigh ina raibh mé ag smaointiú ná, 'mas rud é go bhfuil tú sa bheairic beidh tú ag teacht amach ach más rud é go mbéarfaí ort agus rud inteacht i do lámh agat...'...dhéanfainn cinnte nach rachainn ar ais go príosún agus is dócha gurb é sin an dóigh is fearr chun sin a rá. Phós mé agus mé amuigh ag an tréimhse sin agus ansin rugadh orm arís. Bhí mé ag déanamh na moirtéaraí móra sin a bhí againn sna mall-ochtóidí chun ionsaí a dhéanamh ar bheairic Arm na Breataine.

Nuair a tháinig na péas isteach, thuig mé nach gnáthghunnaí an RUC a bhí acu agus thuig mé ansin ar an phointe agus iad ag teacht fríd an doras gurbh iad an shoot to kill squad. Ach bhí mé ag amharc ar shúile an duine seo agus thuig mé nach raibh sé chun mé a mharú. Bhí mé ag smaointiú domh féin, 'an bhfuil tú chun deireadh a chur leis an rud seo?'. Bhí mé buartha dá mbeadh rud é go dtosóinn rud inteacht, sa dóigh nach mbeinn ag gabháil isteach sa phríosún arís, nach mbeadh an bheirt eile ag gabháil isteach sa phríosún agus níorbh é sin cinneadh s'agamsa le déanamh. Ar feadh soicind ansin bhí mé idir dhá comhairle, 'right, cad é atá tú ag déanamh anseo? An bhfuil tú ag gabháil ar ais go príosún? Right, ok, bhuel má tá tú ag gabháil ar ais go príosún bhuel sin é'.

Are you going back to prison?
Seanna Breathnach

I was determined not to go back to prison. I had been caught red-handed three times, not once or twice but three times. I knew they couldn't break me under interrogation. The way I thought about it was, 'If you are in the barracks you will come out but if you are captured with something in your hand...' I would make sure not to go back to prison and that's probably the best way to say it.

I got married while I was out at that time and then I was caught again. I was making those big mortars that we had in the late-80s to attacks British Army barracks. When the police came in I realised that they didn't have the usual RUC weapons, and I understood on the spot as they came through the door that they were the shoot-to-kill squad. But I was looking into this man's eyes and I realised that he wasn't going to kill me. I was thinking to myself, 'Are you going to put an end to all this?' I was worried that if I started something, so that I wouldn't go back to jail again, that the other two wouldn't go to jail and that wasn't my decision to make. For a second there I was in two minds, 'Right, what are you doing here? Are you going back to prison? Right, okay, well if you are going back to jail then that's it.'

100 **Because you were mixed you were worried**
Jayne Davidson

When you think of the old streets they were just big, long, streets. It changed then when the area all got rebuilt. I had been moved into Cliftondene in a temporary house, and then I bought a house up the street. Cliftondene was mixed, I had a Catholic family on one side and I had a grand master from the Orange Order on the other side of me. I was happy there but when any sort of trouble flared up, or anything happened, it didn't matter what, because you were mixed you were worried. I was always conscious when my kids were out at night, because my son hung about Ballysillan I'd have said, 'is he either going to get a kicking from the other side or could it be someone of his own side kicking him thinking he's from….' So I was always aware and saying to myself, 'He could get it from both parties because he's going into a mixed area'. And I can remember my daughter one time coming in from the Spar, and she'd cut down Cliftondene Gardens to get into Cliftondene Crescent, and I can remember the squeals, and me running out and there was her running down. They used to congregate at the Spar and she had been chased. So I was always saying to myself, 'Maybe I should make a stand here and move to where my identity is known to be of one side or the other'. And you know, I was quite happy there, and to be honest I would have said my Catholic neighbour was a better neighbour to me than what my own side would have been. But that particular time, I said to myself, 'I wonder should I move away. Should I move either into Alliance again where I am known to be, because this isn't working? It's certainly not working for my kids.

101 Everybody had nick-names
Sean Carmichael

You've a guy called Forty Hankies because he's always gurning. You've a guy called Forty Coats. There's Bobby Bus-stop. One of the mechanics, Paul Leonard, God rest him he's dead now, used to call Jim Neeson 'Dickie Rock' because he used to think he was a button for Dickie Rock, and Neeson hated it but it stuck with Jim for years. Anybody that was going up to see him, Paul would say, 'You're going up to see Dickie Rock, are you? Tell him I was asking about him.' The same as old Paddy Mulvenna, they called him Mussolini because of the big eyebrows and all. Everybody had nick-names. Everybody.

102 One of the starkest things
Johnston Price

The decision to live in the Lower Ormeau became very important to me as I had there the sense of community that I had lost in Stranmillis as Stranmillis changed. It was a mix that suited me. Also what became important was that Fionn, my son, was born in '95. So we became even more integrated with the community, not in a deliberate kind of way, just having a child connects you to your neighbours and people around you. It's enormous credit to my family because when you do grow up in a particular community and you take on a set of values and beliefs that are different to the community, it does bring its pressures. And I've always tended to make light of those but only because, in a sense, I've been able to impose upon my family. You know, my brother was a bit surprised at Fionn being called Fionn. I think he would say he's very much at ease with that now. But, even more surprised, then, when Fionn started to be educated through Irish. There was a naiscoil just round the corner so Fionn joined the naiscoil and then went into the bunscoil in An Droichead. But the most difficult thing for my brother was me being caught up in the marching thing in the Lower Ormeau. I wasn't one of the organisers but I took part in the protests. You'd appear on TV and my brother would have been working on the Shankill at the time and certainly would have had very unpleasant things said to him. But he's always been a very personable character and a strong character and he would just turn round and say, 'You know, that big fella, he's is a bit of a eejit.' What else do you say in those sort of circumstances? But he managed to cope with all that.

A lot of the anger in the community was about how some of the Orange marchers had behaved following the bookies killings. Probably one of the most striking experiences of my life was just the day that the bookies killings took place. I know where I was. I was up Glengormley direction through work. They were trying to track me down as much through work as through Maggie. Because it wouldn't have been unknown for me to go into the bookies. But it's really hard to find the words for it. It was just like a real sort of cloud of death, just a pallor or something about the whole area… The quietness of the street was amazing because there were always kids in the street. It was full of kids all the time. It's certainly one of the starkest things I ever remember. I wasn't in any way close to any of the victims, but I knew some of them, particularly one of the young fellas, Peter Magee. I always played golf and I used to give him some golf balls.

103 Bunadh na Cultúrlainne agus Coláiste Feirste
Séamus Mac Seáin

Deich mbliana i ndiaidh deireadh a bheith leis an chéad mheánscoil i 1989, a bhí á teagasc ag Pádraig Ó Maolchraoibhe, Fionnbarr Diamond agus daoine eile, tháinig Gearóid Ó Cairealláin chun tosaigh. Bhí páiste s'aige i ndiaidh toiseacht ar an bhunscoil agus é féin agus a bhean, Aoife, ag an am, dúirt siadsan, 'bhuel, tá rud amháin cinnte, níl páistí s'againne ag gabháil chuig meánscoil Bhéarla', mar sin de, thosaigh siadsan ansin ag smaointiú ar mheánscoil a bhunú. Tháinig siad chugam ó tharla go raibh baint agam leis an chéad cheann agus go raibh ceachtanna áirithe foghlamtha agam faoin rud agus d'iarr siad orm a bheith bainteach leis an darna iarracht.

Thosaigh muid amach i 1989, bhailigh muid roinnt airgid le chéile. Leis an fhírinne a rá, Pádraig Ó Maolchraoibhe agus Malachy Duffin a bhailigh an chuid is mó den airgead sin. Bhailigh muid £11,000 - sin airgead cúpla mí do bheirt mhúinteoirí agus d'fhógair muid go raibh muid ag gabháil a bhunú scoile. Níor éirigh linn é a bhunú i 1990, ach d'éirigh linn é bhunú i 1991. Ní raibh muid cinnte, ní raibh ach beirt mhúinteoirí cáilithe againn, Fergus Ó hÍr agus Cathal Ó Donnghaile. Ní raibh muid cinnte cá mbeadh sé lonnaithe fiú amháin, cé go raibh leathshocrú déanta go mbeadh sé i gCumann Chluain Árd. Ach, chuala mise go raibh an áit seo (An Chultúrlann) le bheith ar fáil. A fhad agus go dtiocfadh leo a chruthú don Springfield Charitable Association go dtiocfadh leo leas a bhaint as ar son an phobail. So, shuigh mé féin, Gearóid Ó Cairealláin agus Liam Andrews síos, scríobh muid ar chúl bileoige ag an Coffee House, thuas i mBaile Andarsan, ag rá cad é an rud a ba mhaith linn a fheiceáil. Ba mhaith linn seo, siúd agus an rud eile le bheith ann. Ach, is ar son na meánscoile a bhí sé. Ní raibh ann ach naonúr páistí agus ní raibh ach rang amháin de dhíth orainn. Bhí an áit ollmhór, tá 14,000 troithe cearnach ann. Agus b'éigean dúinn a rá, 'bhuel, ba mhaith linn go mbeadh amharclann ann, ba mhaith linn go mbeadh siopa ann, ba mhaith linn go mbeadh caifé ann, ba mhaith linn seo siúd agus eile' agus chuaigh muid chucu agus dúirt muid, 'sin an rud a ba linn a fheiceáil ann'. Dar ndóighe, bhí cúlra againn, bhí muid i ndiaidh scoil a bhunú, bhí muid i ndiaidh bunscoil iomlán mór a thógáil, bhí muid i ndiaidh Bombay Street a atógáil, bhí muid i ndiaidh Eastát Tionsclaíochta na Carraige Báine a thógáil, bhí muid i ndiaidh a lán rudaí a dhéanamh. Mar sin, bhí cúlra againn. Agus sin mar a thosaigh sé.

The Establishment of the Cultúrlann and Coláiste Feirste
Séamus Mac Seáin

Ten years after the first secondary school came to an end, in 1989, which had been taught by Pádraig Ó Maolchraoibhe, Fionnbar Dynan and others. Gearóid Ó Cairealláin came forward. His children had just started at the Bunscoil and he and his wife at the time, Aoife, they said, 'Well, one thing's for sure, our children are not going to an English-language secondary school.' And so they started thinking then about setting up a secondary school. They came to me since I was involved in the first one and I had learnt some lessons about it and they asked me to be involved in the second effort.

We started out in 1989 and collected some money. To tell the truth, Pádraig Ó Maolchraoibhe and Malachy Duffin collected most of that money. We raised £11,000 – that was a few months' money for two teachers and we announced that we were going to establish a school. We weren't able to set it up in 1990, but we did in 1991. We weren't sure, we only had two qualified teachers, Fergus Ó hÍr and Cathal Ó Donnghaile. We weren't even sure where the school would be situated, although we had half-arranged that it would be in Cumann Chluain Ard. But I heard that this place (An Chultúrlann) was available. As long as we could prove to the Springfield Charitable Association that they could make it beneficial for the community. So I sat down with Gearóid Ó Caireallán and Liam Andrews, we wrote on the back of a leaflet in the Coffee House up in Andersonstown saying what we wanted to see in the place. We wanted this, that and the other to be in it. But it was for the Meánscoil. There were only nine pupils and we only needed one class. The place was massive, it has 14,000 square feet. And we had to say, 'Well, we want there to be a theatre, we want to have a shop, we want to have a café, we want this and that' and we went to them and said, 'This is what we want to see in it.' Of course, we had a background, we had established a school, we had built a large bunscoil, we had rebuilt Bombay Street, we had built the Whiterock Industrial Estate, we had done a lot of things. So we had a background. And what's how it started.

104 **Remembering Brendan Ormsby**
Joe Burns

Brendan Ormsby was a self-taught mechanic and he kept the fleet on the road. The first time I met him he actually told me what he done. He was a milkman and he read the books about what to do with mechanics and stuff like that, so he was a self-taught mechanic. But the things that he used to do! I remember one time he came to me and he says to me, 'Joe you're the very man I want to have a talk with, you know everything about the building'. I says, 'yes, I know most of it. I can't turn around and tell you I know a hundred per cent, but whatever it is I'll let you know'. He says, 'I'm building a boiler'. I said, 'what kind of a boiler?' He says, 'a boiler that you put into the fire and it heats up the water'. I says, 'how are you doing that?' 'Oh', he says, 'this stuff that I'm getting is the stuff that they use for the rockets going to the moon.' He says, 'it is going to heat up forty or fifty times quicker than the conventional boiler there now'. And he said, 'me and Jim Neeson are going on the whack'. So when I went into the committee meeting I said to Jim, 'here, are you going on the whack with Brendan?' He says, 'what for?' I said, 'the boilers'. He said, 'friggin sure I'm not, there's no way I would go near it'. That was Brendan, he was a character in himself, you know.

105 **Operation Tonnage**
Lee Lavis

One of the last major operations carried out by the British Army was called Operation Tonnage, which was the rebuilding and reinforcing of Crossmaglen and Forkhill police stations – a massive operation. All the equipment had to

101

be moved down from the engineer's base at Antrim – the Royal Engineers - because you couldn't get civilian engineers and contractors in to do that kind of work. Our whole company and two other companies were flown into Bessbrook Mill, and then from Bessbrook Mill we were placed along one of the entry routes to Crossmaglen. We were there for three days, and half of our troops dug in little trenches at the side of the road and the rest of the troops were patrolling around them. What we were doing was guarding the route. It was so dangerous as nothing had been moved by roads in South Armagh since the mid-1970s. It had all been moved by air since. It was just too dangerous to move by roads. So you had to get three companies of troops, that's 250 British soldiers, who dug in along the side of the road and then the rest patrolled around us so we could go up the access route. That was for three days. I was in one of the trenches and I can remember the convoy going past. It was literally past me in three minutes. It flew past us and as it did we were then helicoptered into Bessbrook. It sort of collapsed as it went past us. Crossmaglen has four access roads running into a square. They got armoured containers and basically built a semi-permanent checkpoint at every entrance into Crossmaglen, and I was in one of those semi-permanent checkpoints. The whole operation lasted ten weeks. At any one time there could be in excess of 1000 troops carrying out the protection. There were ten attacks in ten weeks. The local south Armagh units weren't going to let it stand that we were there. This was giving them plenty of targets and like I say, ten attacks in ten weeks including the bringing down of a helicopter – it was hard graft. This was sort of running from April to July 1994. Now what makes me angry about all this in hindsight is that this was happening between April and July 1994. The first ceasefire was announced on August 31st 1994. This has been on the cards for two years, and there had been negotiations going on and so on, and with all this on the cards, they put us on the ground. Put our lives at risk, never mind what it did to the local population in terms of radicalising them with a peace process coming up. And the cost - massive cost. And it was done knowing that the ceasefire was imminent. Surely it would have been better to not risk the lives, the imposition on the local population, and the saving of money.

106 **You started to realise Protestant and Catholic didn't really get on too well**
Mark Anderson

I started off in Holywood Primary, and then I went to Holywood High School. I think it was High School that you started to realise Protestant and Catholic didn't really get on too well. You started learning a bit about the troubles. You would hear other people saying, 'He is a wee Fenian'. Or something like that, and you would go, 'What do you mean?' It was strange because Holywood was never like that. I mean, I grew up with Catholic friends. There were Catholic and Protestants, we all ran about together and then high school. Catholic friends were sent to the school that was their religion, which was Columbanus. So you made new friends and sort of distanced yourself from the old friends that you had. At high school you saw that your Protestant friends were your Protestant friends and your Catholic friends, you just didn't have, because they went to a different school. I was always in and around band scenes and things like that whereas my Catholic friends were, 'No, we don't like the bands, they are wick, they're rotten, they shouldn't be here'. So that is when you go to yourself, 'Well maybe I will not knock about with him no more'.

107 Closing the Crumlin Road jail
Andrew Larmour

I am proud to say that I was one of the ones who got Crumlin Road prison closed. It was all about segregation and better jail conditions. One night I came back from a visit and I got told, 'we're going to take the yard. We're not coming back, we're staying in the yard'. There was 105 loyalist prisoners, UVF, Red Hand Commandoes, UDA prisoners, in the Crumlin Road at that stage. The first time ever, by the way, that loyalists had outnumbered republicans in the Crumlin Road jail. There was only 67, I think, republican prisoners.

We all got onto that roof and climbed onto the main roof of the prison. You could see right down onto the Crumlin Road. Eventually the whole 105 of us were on the roof for a protest. We wrecked the roof. After we came down we were told that if we had have pressed further we could have shut the jail there and then. We could have wrecked it and that would have been it. Our main issue was when we got down we weren't to be touched. There was nobody harmed in any way, we were just marched back to our cells.

If we'd have wrecked it they'd have closed it. So the following Saturday night we decided 'right we are gonna just push to close this place.' It was a Victorian prison, it was 100 years old jail conditions.

So at 10 o'clock the next Saturday night… we knew prison officers would have been in their own home environment drinking, so it would have taken them a couple of hours to get a response unit to come into the jail. So at 10 o'clock on the Saturday night, away we went. We bust our bed ends, got metal bars off our bed ends and away we went, digging the walls. Wrecked the place.

108 An educational journey
David Stitt

I got out in 1997, about two years early, as part of the Good Friday Agreement. I got involved again with the organisation. Everything was just mad after the ceasefire. Just in and out of feud after feud. It was a really dangerous time. The most dangerous time of my life. We were feuding with the UVF, then we were feuding with the LVF, then we were feuding internally within the UDA, and then we were feuding with the LVF again. And the guys you were feuding with lived two streets away from you. They knew exactly where you lived, knew where you picked your kids up from school, knew where you shopped. So you were in that type of situation where people that were out to kill you lived really close by. At that time, during the feuds, there were four attempts on my life. It was just a blur but what I can remember is somebody shooting at you, and you're running away and in your head you're going, 'Is that shots? Are they really firing at me?' You can't believe it. You just hear the bang and pops going round you, and your heart starts skipping and you're away like a shot, you're running for your life. They were dangerous times then and it was just power struggles within your own areas. And that's just how it rolled on for years until I started thinking, 'there's more to life than this, than what I'm doing. All I'm doing is inflicting hurt on people within my own community'. And I just started saying to myself, 'there's obviously a different way of doing things'. There was no water-shed moment. I met Frankie Gallagher again and he showed me a way of really effecting change, how to bring change within your community. I was trying to change people's views forcibly, and he showed me a good way of doing it where you have a more lasting effect. It felt good to be doing something good. It just grabbed me. I liked helping people. I got a job in the 'prison to peace programme', and I just went on a sort of journey, an educational journey. I did an access course to university and registered for my degree that September. That was five, six years ago, and I got an honours degree nearly a year ago.

109 **This huge collective sigh of relief**
Lee Lavis

I'll never forget that day as long as I live. I was still an infantryman when the ceasefire was announced so I was still on the streets. There'd been rumblings that this was going to happen, but we didn't live in a world of current affairs and so on, so when it was eventually announced – I was in Newry – I can remember all the cars beeping their horns and there was a really amazing atmosphere amongst the local population. I can remember going out on patrol and we were ordered to put berets on, rather than helmets, and it projects a very, very different image. A helmet, it's a piece of protection but it also projects you as a combat soldier involved in combat. A beret is slightly more informal, and it allows you to become more of an individual, it's much more

revealing of your face and who are, and you've got cap badges that different regiments can be picked out with. I can remember the happiness with which the ceasefire was greeted on the part of the local population, or maybe more the amazement that such a thing had come to pass. I can remember being out on patrol and I started to get asked more conversational questions by adults, 'oh what does your badge mean?' One thing about South Armagh and Newry was that kids didn't interact with you at all but on that ceasefire day they did. I just remember this sort of…just relaxing for that day.

It felt like this huge collective sigh of relief. I can remember the lack of animosity towards us. It was like a ceasefire on animosity. I can remember one guy, who was quite a local character, shouting to us, 'sure it won't be long until you're home now lads'. And in that there was a jag, a kind of joke, but the way it was put forward it was very different to the way that kind of statement would have been put forward to us the day before. It was a massive day and it was a moment that changed me forever, because it was from that moment that I thought that I would have the room to read about the conflict and start learning about the conflict in which I was involved.

110 **It tore my heart out**
Alan Quail

We were in our house, a wee semi, up at the top of Ballyronan for, I would say, about 27 years. And then a feud broke out between the UVF and the UDA. And on the 1st November, 2000, we just got home from work and the wife was hanging out her washing and she says, 'Somebody's kicking our Mark's door.' And I ran out the front, just to see the gunman coming out the front door, running up the street. I ran up the stairs and I can't be sure, but I think Mark was still alive and I just held him. . . . . I think somebody else phoned the police and ambulance service. So I went down and I had to tell my wife. It tore my heart out. Three days later they sent me a death threat. So it ended up we had to get out. So we went to live with my mother in law, up in Skegoneil Avenue, or just off Skegoneil Avenue. And we stayed there until I'd heard a bloke was selling a house down in Mount Vernon. We had to go somewhere where my wife felt safe. Over in my mother in law's I was staying up through the night, and sleeping during the day. It has a terrible effect on your life, and what way you think about living and stuff. Mount Vernon was a small estate, especially when you have come out of a massive estate like we had just lived in.

People's perceptions from outside are, 'Oh. I wouldn't go in there. Bad, bad area.' But, having lived here now from 2001, we have found it brilliant, and the people in it are brilliant. There's still a massive sense of community togetherness in here. Certain newspapers have lambasted Mount Vernon because of its past and because, like any other estates, they were aligned to certain organisations. But the UVF were infiltrated in Mount Vernon and the government have a lot to answer for here too. Because people were let get away with murder and people on the outside saw that. But they tarred everyone with the same brush. And a lot of the stuff that they wrote about the estate just wasn't true.

111 **The wreckage of an entire family**
Tracey Coulter

It started with the Good Friday Agreement. I hate it. Because after the Good Friday Agreement it was like the organisations, the likes of the military commanders and the young bloods, they were all thirsty for fighting with their enemy, but they didn't have their enemy to fight with any more. And obviously it's what they lived and breathed and believed in, and so to me that's when they decided they needed to fight with each other then. So it was like, who can be bigger and better in the organisations between the UDA and the UVF, which at one stage were all the same when they were fighting against the IRA. So you were thinking you were coming out of one thing for it to go into peace, and then you were going right back into the same feelings, only it was for people against each other in your own communities.

It started off with bands. There was this band parade to happen and it took place on the 19th of August. My Daddy was always a bandsman so they put him in charge of that, but he actually wasn't well about a week beforehand. He was having chest pains and they kept him in hospital. So my Daddy actually signed himself out of the hospital to do this parade, because he felt that he couldn't let anybody down and he had all the bands organised, what way they would go from start to finish, and that was fine. But there was still the tension even building up to the parade. And then, obviously, there was quite a lot of all the family members, like brothers of my Daddy, and friends and close family that were also paramilitary connected, and you knew, you were just… you were worried. You knew something was going to happen, and you were just constantly worrying. So the parade went off and it went well. It was a gorgeous day, the sun was beating out of the sky. It was really, really lovely. And the next thing I saw all these people just running, and I mean they were running everywhere. Then after it I learnt that they were passing the Rex bar and one of them threw a bottle, and the next thing there were gun shots fired at the Rex bar, there were people injured, two people were shot I think. And then there was just this eerie feeling. People were getting put out of their homes. Like this was all happening all on the same day. It all just went wild. People that lived there all their lives, their homes were being wrecked, and they were getting put out because they had connections to the UVF, and it was really bad. And I just kept thinking, 'Oh god, this is terrible. This is really bad'.

And then the Sunday was still the same. The road was dead. It was a real bad atmosphere, and I couldn't settle. When my Daddy came in that night I went into my Mammy's, and I was crying my eyes out, and I said, 'I don't want you to stay here Daddy, they're watching you', and he was like, 'No they're not'. And I was like, 'No. Just don't stay. We'll go to my Granny's. Come on'. So we got into my Granny's and my Daddy had sat down, and him and my granda were kind of talking, and he says to my granda, 'God, this is awful. This is just bad', he said. 'This is turning brother against brother, and friend against friend, and no-one wants this'. So I'd left my Daddy there and drove on down and stayed in my Mammy's house with her. And my Daddy rang about twenty past nine the next morning and said, 'I'm coming down now. Tell your Ma to open the door'. And he was talking about it again, 'This is awful', and all. Just before twelve he says, 'Right, I'm going to go and get fags'. And I was like, 'Daddy, please can I go with you? Just let me go with you', and he was, 'Tracey, no. If your time's up, your time's up', and away out the door he went. And then he left the house at about a quarter past twelve, and he was shot dead at half twelve.

Our neighbour Wesley came over to tell us. I opened the door and looked at him and didn't even say, 'What is it?', because I knew that he was going to say something bad. And he just says, 'Your Daddy's been shot'. I run up the street and I just kept running, and it felt like I was running for hours, trying to get to the top of the street. It was lashing down rain, real bad rain that day, and I heard all the ambulance sirens and I saw all these crowds. When I got to the top of the street three people, friends of mine, stopped me and gripped me and wouldn't let me down, and I was squealing and kicking them. 'Let me down, I need to get down to see if my Daddy's down there. Please tell me, is he dead? Is he dead?' And the wee boy that was there, who is actually also dead now, wee Al Mc McCullough, he was crying his eyes out, and he just nodded his head, 'Yes'. And that was it like, that was just the wreckage of an entire family.

112 Drum corps, flute corps, base drummer, leading tip, flags, band pole
John Dougan

I love bands. It annoys me to think of the way people speak of them when they haven't given any time or consideration to the effort that they put in. My wee lad is 18 years of age now. When he was six he got his first flute. Within a year, a year and a half, he was a full blown flute. He ended up joining the Girdwood Star in East Belfast and he's been in it for years. The dedication of him. They practice once a week, every week, except for two weeks of the year. People don't see the amount of dedication and the time that they give. I don't think there is anybody or any group that has a constant, week in, week out, gathering the way they do. Or give themselves to parades. I mean before a band will get a band back into their area, they have to have paraded with the band prior to that. So if my band goes and does 100 parades that year, they expect a hundred bands to return to their parade, each year. The more parades that you do, the more bands you get back into your area. So that shows your commitment. If 50 bands turned up and do a parade on a night on the Shankill then that means you have done 50 parades and they are saying 'thank you'. When they come back then it's about drum corps, flute corps, base drummer, leading tip, flags, band pole, and the competition in all the different things. Whoever wins the drummers and fluters, they get the overall winner. But it's the amount that goes into it that people don't grasp. And I hate at times when I see things written about bands because they haven't a clue.

113 I missed my kids more than anything
Colin Curragh

I ended up in Maghaberry. I went onto the loyalist wing there, in Bush House. I was a bit depressed at the start. But you just have to get on with it, and it wasn't long going in. Looking back, it flew in. Where did them couple of years go? I didn't see them going in. But I missed out on my kids when I was in jail. At that point I had two. I missed my kids more than anything. And that's the only thing that affected me, the kids. In Bush House it was always good craic, always a bit of banter. But I wouldn't want to go back. I wouldn't want to miss out on any more of my kids' lives. I have three kids now. I have a wee lad, he is 15. My wee girl is 10, and the youngest she's only turned one. Seeing this new wee one here growing up and all, I say, 'I didn't see that there with the other two'. I missed out on my other two, and I don't want to do that on her.

114 Scouts, work or church?
Irene Glassey

I go to church on a Sunday morning or a Sunday night. I take Sunday school. I take scouts and, you know, I believe in my faith. My faith keeps me going. And I'm a social person. I'd be wanting to see what I can do for my community. I love my job because I work in the community. I would hate to have to go back to working in Mackie's again behind a desk in an office. Because I'd be out and somebody would say, 'Hello' and Joe would say to me, 'Scouts, work or church? Which one?' and I'd say that one's scouts, the other one was church, and this one's work. So I just love working in the community and I do love my job, most of the time.

115 I started putting dialogue to the thoughts
Robert Niblock

I went in to Long Kesh in January 1973 as a 17 year-old. In April I escaped and was caught and I got a further seven months added onto my sentence. I was due for release in March 1975, and on the day of my release I was re-arrested at the gate and charged with a murder, and taken straight back in again. I got out in 1990. I came out as a 34 year-old. I had 17 years free and 17 years in prison. It took me a long time to adjust. My mother and father had both died while I had been in and I went to stay with my older sister. After a while I was able to get a place of my own, and that presented difficulties too because I knew nothing about practical things. When I was earning money I had no bank account, so any money I had I kept in a drawer in the house, and it ended up my brother-in-law had to go and open up a bank account for me. I didn't know how to do that. I didn't know about insurance or phoning the tax office or whatever. It was something that had to be learned. Coming out, you were sort of like a child, you were helpless in many ways.

I always had an interest in writing and a great interest in reading. Probably one of the biggest regrets I have is that I didn't write any more in all the time I was in prison. When I came out I was too busy trying to get life back on track and stuff like that, although I continued to read a lot. It wasn't until the late '90s/early 2000s that I started writing short stories and wee set pieces and things like that. I never had a notion of writing a play. But in 2008 I had a friend who was diagnosed as having terminal cancer, and he was one of these guys who was the life and soul of the party. He was very, very, fun-loving, a good laugh, brilliant joker. But it showed me another side to him because he made it known that he didn't want people to come up and see him because he was dying. I had met him at a wee charity function just before he died and he said to me, 'Look, you know, you probably never thought you'd hear me saying this, but I can't deal with this here at all. People think I'm so happy-go-lucky, but there is a different side here and that's what I don't want people to see.'

So it sort of got me thinking and I started scribbling down a few ideas and, for some reason, I started putting dialogue to the thoughts. And then it developed from there really, and I had this idea around someone learning that they have a terminal illness. I turned that into two people having a terminal illness, two friends, and wrote a comedy around the serious subject of terminal cancer. I gave it out to a few people to read. One of the people I gave it to was a freelance writer and she contacted me and said, 'Look, I think this is quite good. Do you want to meet?' Basically it went from there, so knowing that I could write, and write at a half decent level, spurred me on a wee bit and so I just continued writing. It's something I enjoy doing now and maybe I find it a wee bit therapeutic.

116 **Caithfidh fís a bheith agat**
Marcas Mac Ruairí

An ghlúin nó an piargrúpa más maith leat lena raibh mé, ní raibh meas acu ar an stát. De bharr nach raibh meas ag daoine ar an stát, ní raibh meas acu ar aon rud a tháinig ón stát. Mar shampla, bheadh daoine ag briseadh an dlí. Níl polaitíocht ar bith le goideadh, ag briseadh isteach, ach margadh dubh agus smuigleáil ann. Ní raibh drochmheas ag daoine ar an mhargadh dubh, de bharr nach raibh meas acu ar an stát.

Nuair a tháinig na stailceanna ocrais chun tosaigh, ba léir go raibh sé bunaithe ar chur in iúl don saol mór an streachailt ar son cothromais agus ar son neamhspleáchas Éireann. Ba rud polaitiúil é. Chuidigh sé sin liom, i m'intinn féin, difear a dhéanamh. Níor leor drochmheas a bheith agat ar an stát. Bhí fís dhearfach de dhíth faoin rud a bhí tú chun cur in áit an stáit. Chuidigh an feachtas in éadan na mblocanna H agus na stailceanna ocrais. Rinne sé sin soiléir i m'intinn nach leor a bheith ag cur in éadan an stáit ach go gcaithfidh fís a bheith agat don rud a bhí tú chun cur in áit an stáit.

You need to have a vision
Marcas Mac Ruairí

The generation I was with, or the peer group if you like, they had no respect for the state. Because people didn't respect the state, they didn't respect anything that came from the state. For example, people would break the law. Maybe there was no politics to stealing, breaking in and there was smuggling and a kind of black market. People didn't disrespect the black market, because they didn't respect the state.

When the hunger strikes came to the fore, it made clear to the world that the struggle was for justice and the independence of Ireland. It was something political. That helped me sharpen the difference in my mind. It's not enough to disrespect the state. It was necessary to have a positive vision about what you wanted to replace the state. The campaign against the H Blocks and the hunger strikes helped in that way. It made it clear in my mind that it wasn't enough to oppose the state but you had to have a vision for what you were going to put in place of the state.

117 It was going to that meeting and Harold Good
Billy Hutchinson

One of the things that stands out for me about growing up on the Shankill was that there was a lot of ex-military people. We had a family in our street, I think there was six of them, and they were all born in different cities around the world. Their father was in the army and then came home. And these guys didn't have work. They were trying to get work and doing whatever they could to get work, and even going away to England to get work, and they disappeared for a while and then came back again. It was only later on you started to realise that these people had been off fighting, in Korea and Aden and all these types of places, and then came back and there was no work. Once they came out of the army they didn't have a job. And everybody in the area was looking for jobs. I can remember the horn going in Mackie's in the morning and people were running down the street to get to Mackie's in time. You had to get in. They were all rushing to get in before the gate closed. The other thing I remember is women going to work and they went to Edenderry mill and Ewarts mill. And you didn't need a clock, you could tell the time, because you knew what time they were going to work and they were going up or down the street. They all had different shifts. People went around rapping people up to be in time for work.

And as I was growing up they started the slum clearance and the Morgan plan. And I can remember there was a minister in Agnes Street, actually it was Harold Good. Obviously Harold was a young minister at this time. And he came out looking for young people in the street and he said to us all, 'why don't you come into the church?' We were all sceptical, but he got us in this night and he brought these people out and they started asking us questions. It was about what do you think about all this, or what would you like to see? And I can remember there were no baths in people's houses. You got bathed in a tin bath in the yard, or in front of the fire in the winter. And they'd

109

built these showers in Malvern Street because of slum clearance, and people didn't have any baths and St. Peter's Hill's baths had been closed down. You just went for a shower in it and it cost you a shilling. So he was talking to us all about this, and what did we think could be put back into the area. And what do young people want. All that sort of stuff. And I suppose at the time I didn't realise how significant it was, but he was consulting us and asking us what we wanted. And then when I went to prison I read Ron Wieners book about the rape and plunder of the Shankill. I had decided that after doing social sciences I wanted to do town planning, and that's what I did and it was for that reason. It was first of all going to that meeting, and it was Harold Good.

and in many ways a young man's fight. We didn't have all the cogs in the wheels working. Even if someone was working for the welfare they were not as well regarded. And you know if you didn't have somebody doing welfare for the prisoners the whole thing falls down. That recognition that everybody's role is as important as the next person's. We didn't do that. There's loads of work to be done within our communities, and there's not enough people doing it. If you were prepared to lift a bomb or a gun to defend your community then the transition to community development is easy. You know I've heard people in rooms saying, 'I didn't join the UVF to do community development.' Well I don't think Martin McGuinness joined the IRA to do what he's now doing. Things move, things change, things evolve and you have to keep up with it.

118 **The cogs in the wheel**
Raymond Laverty

We don't use role models from within the movements. We have lots of people who fought the fight that people would know and respect. We don't utilise them to get us moving forward. People can say, 'Well I can listen to that person because I know that they've been there and done that. And if they're saying this, it must be the right way to go.' And it takes away that thing of young people thinking they're missing out on something.

Maybe one of the differences with the republican movement is that when they were fighting the fight, they also were doing community development. The loyalist side was a very military type fight. Even though there were women who went to prison they're never really mentioned, they're never held up. But there were women. It was seen as a man's fight,

PROCESS

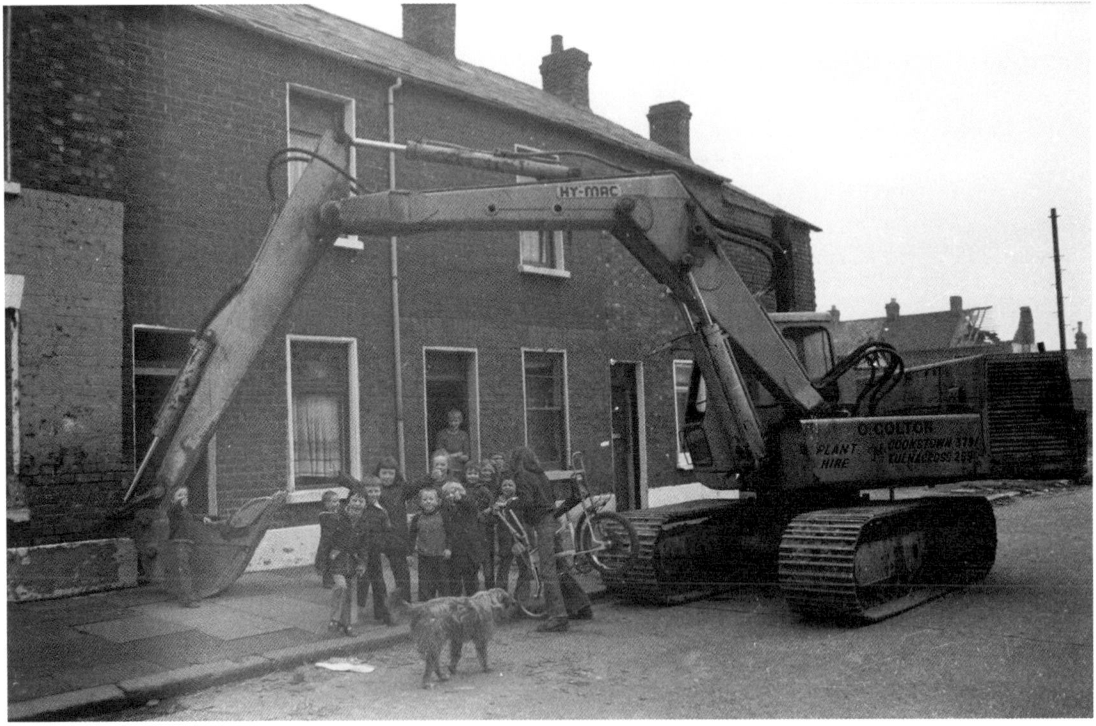
HY-MAC
O COLTON
PLANT
HIRE

LIVING THROUGH THE CONFLICT
Belfast oral histories

PROCESS

This book is the result of a collaborative process involving over 150 people throughout the two and a half years of the project from 2012 to 2014. Three groups of people have been working consistently on the project from the beginning: the staff, the steering group and the interviewers. Each of these layers of the Pieces of the Past project has involved work across political and community differences and divisions. Gathering oral history interviews from people in communities divided by a violent and protracted conflict has been challenging and complex but also stimulating and rewarding as the statements below from the interviewers demonstrate.

At the beginning of the project the steering group spent several meetings working out a common position on gathering the interviews. Everyone shared a belief in the importance of hearing ordinary people's experiences of living through the conflict and the discussion focussed on how to gather interviews responsibly and in a way that would empower the contributors. There was also a desire to explore differences and gain a deeper understanding of each other. A mission statement was developed which reflected these conversations.

Pieces of the Past is an oral history project that records and archives personal experiences of living through the conflict in communities across Belfast. Shankill Women's Centre, Epic, Forbairt Feirste, Charter NI, Fáilte Feirste Thiar and West Belfast Taxi Association are working with Falls Community Council's Dúchas archive to gather oral history interviews and work across divisions. We believe it is important to collect histories of living through the conflict to affirm the experiences of those most affected, understand each other better and leave a legacy to the future.

The steering group meetings were rotated around the offices of the different partner organisations and this hosting helped us to become familiar with each other. The membership of the steering group changed during the lifetime of the project but all members stayed in contact with the project and continued to promote and support the work. As part of the work we organised a series of public community discussions on historical topics. We felt it was important to explore our history and open up a wider community conversation. The topic of each public event was carefully chosen to challenge us but also to be sensitive to an ongoing context of a history that is contested as well as shared. There were eight public discussions organised in locations in East and West Belfast and each event was attended by between 30 and 90 people.

The role of the partner organisations was very important in establishing trust in the project and enabling the interviews to be gathered. Some of the steering group members themselves gave an interview and this also inspired confidence in potential contributors. Two steering group members did the training and became interviewers. In all, 104 interviews were collected and 97 of these are represented in this book. The interviews were carried out by 17 interviewers including both staff and volunteers. A number of training sessions were organised throughout the project and in one of the last sessions another group joined the process – Shankill Area Social History (SASH). Although they were not part of the formal partnership and steering group of the project SASH made a very important contribution through their participation in the training programme and through the interviews they collected.

The project organised four oral history training days throughout the project as well as a series of follow up meetings for interviewers. The follow up meetings were important in enabling the interviewers to discuss their experience of gathering interviews and learn from each other. The meetings were organised in different community locations and also enabled wider discussions on political views. As with the steering group discussions, this required a willingness to be open, to listen and to work through differences. Twenty eight people came through the training and more than half of these went on to do an interview and take part in the group process. Some people did just one interview and others recorded several. The index at the end lists each contributor with the person who interviewed them and the collection they are part of.

The development of the Dúchas oral history archive to create collections from each partner was very significant. The visitor can now search for interviews in, for example, the Shankill Women's Centre collection or if they call up an interview from the list of contributor names they can see to which collection the interview belongs. This gives the partnership of the Pieces of the Past project a lasting presence in the Dúchas archive. It also demonstrates the partner organisations' confidence in the archive and facilitates the individual contributors' ongoing relationship to the Dúchas archive.

The staff were employed by Falls Community Council on the project were:
Project manager Claire Hackett, co-ordinators Lisa Moody and William Mitchell who worked part-time and finance administrator Hayley Gordon.

The people involved in the project steering group over the two and a half years of the project were:
From Belfast Taxis CIC
Eddie Fay and Stephen Savage
From Charter NI
Mark Anderson, Louis Cowan, Jackie McBurney, Billy Rowan, David Stitt and Sam White.
From Epic
Winston Irvine and Tom Roberts
From Fáilte Feirste Thiar
Harry Connolly
From Forbairt Feirste
Jake Mac Siacais
From Shankill Women's Centre
Betty Carlisle and Roberta Gray

The volunteers who carried out interviews were Joe Austin, Janice Chambers, Hugh Corcoran, John Dougan, Lisa Faulkner, Tommy Harrison, Bill Henry, Jackie McBurney, Joan Mercer, Feargal Mac Ionnrachtaigh, Marty McKiernan and Billy Rowan. Below are their statements.

Joe Austin
If we are to understand who we are, then we need to know where we came from. Our project gives a unique oral history of our times and times past.

Janice Chambers
I liked the cross-community aspect of the project, the interaction with the whole group involved and meeting people with a shared interest in our country's history. I loved listening to some wonderful interviews too.

Hugh Corcoran
Is é an caidreamh ar ndearnú idir mé agus na agallaí; scéaltaí daonna s'acu, lán de contrárthachtaí, bród, féinacht, íobairt, spaoi, iontas agus grá. Is pléisiúr agus tairbhe atá bainte agam agus mé ag éisteach, ag cosaint agus ag athléiriú na scéaltaí seo.

> What I liked most about being part of this project was the interaction with interviewees, their human stories, full of contradictions, pride, ego, sacrifice, fun, surprise and love. The experience I have gained from listening to these stories and the responsibility entrusted in me to re-produce and protect them is invaluable.

Johnny Dougan
It was good to learn how to compile narratives so as to build an archive of the rich stories about

our past, particularly with those I interviewed from the Shankill, and to share these stories with others.

Lisa Faulkner
The group of former loyalist political prisoners that I interviewed gave me a greater insight into their life histories and in learning of their experiences I found that I could empathise with them.

Tommy Harrison
I really enjoyed doing Pieces of the Past interviews and would love to continue. I feel that for too long people in and around the Shankill area have been too quiet and wanting to keep things to themselves. The people I interviewed agreed that there are far too many hidden stories that need to be told and preserved in our own archives. I enjoyed interviewing people who were brought up in the Shankill area before the start of the conflict and I wasn't surprised to hear that they had Catholic friends whom they hung about with, drank with and went to dances together. During the interviews I could see the changes in people's faces, in their expression and body language when it came to talking about the start of the conflict. A sort of fear had crept in to the interview and coming to the end of the interview they seemed to be still cautious and sceptical although a ceasefire is now in place. But I understood that, after what these people and many others went through. What pleased me the most was that after each interview the person felt relieved as if they were getting a weight off their chest. This is why I feel we should continue with Pieces of the Past interviews as people are dying and their stories have so much to tell our younger generation.

Bill Henry
I got the opportunity to interview people whose experiences and memories of their lives will live on in an archive long after they have gone.

Joan Mercer
Taking part in the Pieces of the Past project has changed my understanding and appreciation, of how just living life during the 'Troubles' was traumatising and charged with emotion for all involved. Listening to the interviewees and their experiences humbled me, and made me thankful for my own family. We all share this common bond of loving, living and surviving during extreme circumstances, where man inflicts pain and sorrow on fellow humans.

Feargal Mac Ionnrachtaigh
Thaitin sé go mór liom bheith páirteach sa tionscadal 'Pieces of the Past'. Thug sé deis dom stair an phobail a bhailiú ón bhun aníos agus guth a thabhairt dóibh siúd atá imeallaithe ón insint oifigiúil staire. I gcás Forbairt Feirste, bhí lúcháir orainn go bhfuair muid seans scéaltaí spreagúla a bhailiú ó Ghaeil cheannródaíocha a d'imir ról claochlaitheach in athbheochan na Gaeilge agus in athghiniúint pobail in Iarthar Bhéal Feirste i gcoitinne.'

'I really enjoyed participating in the 'Pieces of the Past' project. It gave me the opportunity to collect a 'people's history' and record the view from below by giving voice to those marginalised from the 'official' historical narrative. For our part, Forbairt Feirste felt privileged to have the chance to collect inspirational stories from pioneering Gaels who played a transformational role in the Irish language revival and the regeneration of West Belfast.

Jackie McBurney

The oral history let me see and share the stories that people could only keep to themselves before. Often people thought that they didn't have stories to tell but when we began they found that they did. The interviews brought them back to their early lives. Afterwards I realised that people couldn't wait to show their interviews to their friends and families and that showed me the importance of the work.

Marty McKiernan

What I liked most about being part of this project was meeting different people and hearing different stories. It was very interesting how people saw the same set of events in a different way.

Billy Rowan

So much has been written about the Troubles from academics etc that it just seemed so false and far away. I wanted to read about real people, real lives of people growing up through the Troubles, so to actually be trained and get the chance to interview and have my interviews in print has been absolutely amazing. Here is to all the people who took part. Thank you.

INDEX

FALLS
COMMUNITY COUNCIL
ENTERPRISE AND DEVELOPMENT CENTRE

LIVING THROUGH THE CONFLICT
Belfast oral histories

INDEX OF CONTRIBUTORS
AND INTERVIEWERS

CONTRIBUTOR
INTERVIEWER   **GROUP**

Mark Anderson
Billy Rowan   *Charter NI*

Samuel Aughey
John Dougan   *Shankill Area Social History*

Anne Barkley
Lisa Moody   *Dúchas*

Eileen Bell
Janice Chambers   *Shankill Women's Centre*

Jean Boyce
Bill Henry   *Shankill Area Social History*

Seanna Breathnach
Hugh Corcoran   *Forbairt Feirste*

Danny Brown
Hugh Corcoran   *Forbairt Feirste*

Breige Brownlee
Joe Austin   *Belfast Taxis CIC*

Joe Burns
Joe Austin   *Belfast Taxis CIC*

SeanCarmichael
Joe Austin   *Belfast Taxis CIC*

Kevin Carson
Marty McKiernan   *Dúchas*

David Colvin
Tom Harrison   *Epic*

Bobby Connolly
Joe Austin   *Belfast Taxis CIC*

Tracey Coulter
Joan Mercer   *Shankill Women's Centre*

Geraldine Crawford
Joe Austin *Belfast Taxis CIC*

Colin Curragh
Billy Rowan *Charter NI*

Jayne Davidson
Joan Mercer *Shankill Women's Centre*

Kieran Devlin
Marty McKiernan *Belfast Taxis CIC*

Owen Doherty
Joe Austin *Belfast Taxis CIC*

John Dougan
William Mitchell *Shankill Area Social History*

Beatrice Elliott
Tom Harrison *Epic*

Harry Enright
Feargal Mac Ionnrachtaigh *Dúchas*

Seamus Finucane
Joe Austin *Dúchas*

Gerry Fitzpatrick
Marty McKiernan *Dúchas*

Micky Gallagher
Marty McKiernan *Dúchas*

Sandra Gibney
John Dougan *Shankill Area Social History*

Irene Glassey
Joan Mercer *Shankill Women's Centre*

Liz Groves
Marty McKiernan *Dúchas*

Roy Harris
Jackie McBurney *Charter NI*

Tom Harrison
Jimmy Linton *Epic*

Jo-Ann Harrison
Tom Harrison *Epic*

Ann Henry
Bill Henry *Shankill Area Social History*

Jackie Henry
Bill Henry *Shankill Area Social History*

Bill Henry
William Mitchell *Shankill Area Social History*

Ruby Hill
Jackie McBurney *Charter NI*

Norman Hunt
William Mitchell *Shankill Area Social History*

Billy Hutchinson
Lisa Faulkner *Epic*

Joan Johnston
Janice Chambers *Shankill Women's Centre*

Drew Johnston
John Dougan *Shankill Area Social History*

Jake Kane
Tom Harrison *Epic*

Mary Kelly
Joan Mercer *Shankill Women's Centre*

Ally Kennedy
Jackie McBurney *Charter NI*

Eddie Kinner
Lisa Faulkner *Epic*

Andrew Larmour
Billy Rowan *Charter NI*

Raymond Laverty
Lisa Faulkner *Epic*

Lee Lavis
Claire Hackett *Dúchas*

Joan Linhart
Joan Mercer *Shankill Women's Centre*

Minnie Long
Jackie McBurney *Charter NI*

Terry Lyons
Joe Austin *Belfast Taxis CIC*

Caoimhín Mac Mathúna
Piarsais McAllister *Forbairt Feirste*

Marcus Mac Ruairaí
Hugh Corcoran *Forbairt Feirste*

Séamus Mac Seáin
Hugh Corcoran *Forbairt Feirste*

Seán Mac Seáin
Hugh Corcoran *Forbairt Feirste*

Jake Mac Siacais
Hugh Corcoran *Forbairt Feirste*

Seán Mac Aindreasa
Hugh Corcoran *Forbairt Feirste*

Seán Mag Uidhir
Hugh Corcoran *Forbairt Feirste*

Seán Magaoill
Feargal Mac Ionnrachtaigh *Forbairt Feirste*

Larry Mc Gurk
Hugh Corcoran *Forbairt Feirste*

Jim McAuley
John Dougan *Shankill Area Social History*

Donna McIlroy
Joan Mercer *Shankill Women's Centre*

Norman McMaster
Jackie McBurney *Charter NI*

Alan McVeigh
Jackie McBurney *Charter NI*

Brighid Mhic Sheáin
Hugh Corcoran *Forbairt Feirste*

Máire Mhic Sheáin
Hugh Corcoran *Forbairt Feirste*

Caitlín Mhistéil
Feargal Mac Ionnrachtaigh *Forbairt Feirste*

William Mitchell
Lisa Faulkner *Epic*

Hugh Mornin
Jackie McBurney *Charter NI*

Betty Morrison
Janice Chambers *Shankill Women's Centre*

Paddy Mulvenna
Joe Austin *Belfast Taxis CIC*

Jim Neeson
Joe Austin *Belfast Taxis CIC*

Robert Niblock
Lisa Faulkner *Epic*

Gearóid Ó Cairealláin
Hugh Corcoran *Forbairt Feirste*

Peadar Ó Cuinneagain
Hugh Corcoran *Forbairt Feirste*

Liam Ó Maolchloiche
Hugh Corcoran *Forbairt Feirste*

Pilib Ó Ruanaí
Hugh Corcoran *Forbairt Feirste*

Stevie O Reilly
Joe Austin *Belfast Taxis CIC*

May Paul
Joan Mercer *Shankill Women's Centre*

Michael Pike
Claire Hackett *Dúchas*

Johnston Price
Claire Hackett *Dúchas*

Alan Quail
William Mitchell *Epic*

James Rea
Billy Rowan *Charter NI*

Seamus Rice
Joe Austin *Belfast Taxis CIC*

Paul Rooney
Joe Austin *Belfast Taxis CIC*

Sean Simpson
Marty McKiernan *Dúchas*

Margaret Smith
Joan Mercer *Shankill Women's Centre*

Donna Spence
Jackie McBurney *Charter NI*

Kay Spence
Joan Mercer *Shankill Women's Centre*

Ann Stevenson
Joan Mercer *Shankill Women's Centre*

David Stitt
Jackie McBurney *Charter NI*

Florence Stockman
Bill Henry *Shankill Area Social History*

Charlie Tully
Marty McKiernan *Dúchas*

Jackie Upton
Billy Rowan *Charter NI*

Susie Vallely
Jim Moody   *Dúchas*

Jim Watson
William Mitchell   *Shankill Area Social History*

Jim Watt
Lisa Faulkner   *Epic*

Jude Whyte
Marty McKiernan   *Dúchas*

Rachel Wylie
Janice Chambers   *Shankill Women's Centre*

Acknowledgements

Pieces of the Past is a project supported by the European Union's PEACE III Programme managed by the Special EU Programmes Body. Thanks to Graham Parkinson and Patricia Armstrong from SEUPB for their support.

Anne Carr, Frankie Gallagher and Winston Irvine for their support for the project at an early stage.

The project steering group: Mark Anderson, Betty Carlisle, Harry Connolly, Louis Cowan, Eddie Fay, Roberta Gray, Winston Irvine, Jake Mac Siacais, Jackie McBurney Tom Roberts, Billy Rowan, Stephen Savage, David Stitt and Sam White.

The project staff: Co-ordinators Lisa Moody and William Mitchell who guided and supported the interviewing process and archived the completed interviews. Lily Doran our intern from Duke University in Georgia who contributed to the archiving at just the right time. Hayley Gordon for her meticulous finance and administration work on the project.

The interviewers: Joe Austin, Janice Chambers, Hugh Corcoran, John Dougan
Lisa Faulkner, Tommy Harrison, Bill Henry, William Mitchell, Lisa Moody, Jim Moody, Joan Mercer, Feargal Mac Ionnrachtaigh, Marty McKiernan, Billy Rowan.

The staff and Board of Falls Community Council for unstinting support.

The partner organisations who supported the work: Belfast Taxis CIC, Charter NI, Epic, Fáilte Feirste Thiar, Forbairt Feirste and Shankill Women's Centre. Also Shankill Area Social History who joined the project to gather interviews in the last year.

The transcribers, Hugh Corcoran, Michaeline Donnelly, Máirtín Mac Gabhann, Aidan McAteer, Ronan McConnell, Robert McMillen, Stephen McKenna, Jacqueline Monahan, Jim Moody, Aoife Níc AnTsaoir, Maire O Hare, translator Ciarán Ó Brolcháin, and proof reader Geraldine Telford.

My co-editors for the Irish language sections of the book, Hugh Corcoran and Feargal Mac Ionnrachtaigh from Forbairt Feirste.

All the contributors who gave an oral history interview for the archive and for this book. Thank you for this gift. And remembering David Colvin who died since he recorded his interview.

Claire Hackett
Pieces of the Past and Dúchas oral history archive, Falls Community Council

European Union
European Regional Development Fund
Investing in your future

A project supported by the European Union's PEACE III Programme managed by the Special EU Programmes Body

PIECES OF THE PAST

dúchas ORAL HISTORY ARCHIVE